MEDIA WIZARDS

A Behind-the-Scenes Look at

Media Manipulations

Catherine Gourley

TWENTY-FIRST CENTURY BOOKS
Brookfield, Connecticut

Many of the designations and slogans used by manufacturers and sellers to distinguish their products are claimed as trademarks. Where those designations and slogans appear in this book and Twenty-First Century Books was aware of a trademark claim, the designations and slogans have been printed in initial capital letters. Twenty-First Century Books has made every effort to identify trademarks in this way.

Published by Twenty-First Century Books
A Division of The Millbrook Press
2 Old New Milford Road
Brookfield, Connecticut 06804
www.millbrookpress.com

Cover photograph courtesy of © The Stock Illustration Source, Inc. (Trenton Stull). Photographs courtesy of Corbis-Bettmann: p. 6; MGM/Archive Photos: p. 9; AP/Wide World Photos: pp. 14, 112; Liaison Agency: pp. 17 (© Gilles Mingasson), 64 (© Eric Sander), 74 (© Spencer Tirey), 79 (© Michael Schwarz); Archive Photos: pp. 22, 54; Corbis: p. 26 (© David Allen); Library of Congress: pp. 28, 33 (both); Ontario Ministry of Health: p. 38 (both); UPI/ Corbis-Bettmann: pp. 46 (top), 118; Procter & Gamble: p. 46 (bottom); Envision: p. 67 (left © Paul Poplis; right © Peter Johansky); Corbis-Bettmann: p. 50; Reuters/Michael Ryan/Archive Photos: p. 57; Pepsico, Inc: p. 61; Photofest: pp. 73, 82, 88; © Titan Sports/Sygma: p. 95 (left); © Sygma/ Andy King: p. 95 (right); The Barnum Museum, Bridgeport, CT: pp. 102 ("Scenes From a Busy Life", Lithograph, c. 1881, Strobridge Lithograph Company), 107 (The American Museum, Lithograph, 1850, printed by C. W. Lewis); Archive Photos/Blank Archives: p. 108.

Library of Congress Cataloging-in-Publication Data
Gourley, Catherine, 1950–
Media wizards: a behind-the-scene look at media manipulations / Catherine Gourley.
p.   cm.
Summary: Explores the various tools advertisers, broadcasters, and others involved in the media use to impart messages to the public, describing both historical and contemporary media events and phenomena.
ISBN 0-7613-0967-5 (lib. bdg.)
1. Mass media. 2. Manipulative behavior. [1. Mass media.] I. Title.
P90.G65   1999
302.23—dc21   99-17741   CIP

CONTENTS

Introduction
THE NECROMANCER 7

THE WIZARD'S LANGUAGE
Learning the Media Code Words 11

JIMMY'S WORLD
Crossing the Line From Fact to Fiction 15

MEDIA'S LITTLE WHITE LIES
Sound Bites and Bias 21

AFTER THE BATTLE
Photojournalism at Gettysburg 29

THE METAPHOR IS THE MESSAGE
Using Symbolism in a Public Service
Announcement 35

ADVERTISING FICTIONS
Advertising and Marketing Wizardry 41

CAUGHT IN THE PRESS AGENT'S CROSSHAIRS
Targeting an Audience 44

HERE COMES SANTA CLAUS
How Copywriters and Marketers Celebrate
the Holidays 53

FIVE WAYS TO WANT
Recognizing Advertising Subtexts 59

THE WEASELS
Advertising and the Law 65

JOLTS PER MINUTE
Media's Scare 'n Suspense Tactics 71

FRAMING VIOLENCE IN JONESBORO
Episodic Versus Thematic News Frames 75

SCARE TACTICS
How Infotainment Packages News as Stories 82

BLOOD 'N GUTS 'N LIQUID PLASTIC
Creating Reality on TV's *ER* 89

RAGE IN A CAGE
How Sports, Stereotypes, and Soap Opera Butt Heads
in the Big Ring 93

Part Four

SMOKE AND MIRRORS
Urban Legends and Media Hoaxes 99

THE PRINCE OF HUMBUG
How P. T. Barnum Hoodwinked the World 103

MUTANT CHICKENS, CHOCOLATE CHIP COOKIES, AND SPAM
The Serious and Not-So-Serious Side
of Media Hoaxes 111

BACK TO BARNUM: WHO ARE THE TASADY?
Why "Wish News" Gets Ink 117

Epilogue
CHILDREN FROM HIS BRAIN 121

Chapter Notes 123

Selected Sources 124

Index 127

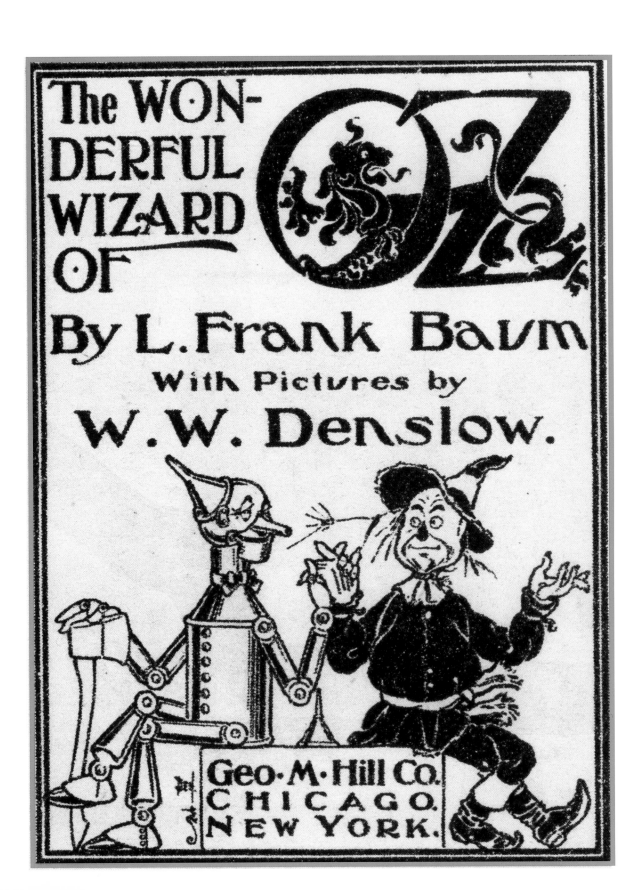

THE NECROMANCER

Hear me, fear me! Never dare to jeer me!
I'm the greatest necromancer ever was!
All my deeds with magic reek,
I'm the whole thing, so to speak!
I'm the Wonderful Wizard of Oz!

from the first unpublished dramatization
of L. Frank Baum's story, 1900

The dream was always the same.
Terrified, the boy runs across a field. Chasing him is a scarecrow. Just as its ragged hay fingers are about to seize the boy's neck, the monster collapses at his feet. The scarecrow was just a lifeless pile of husks, after all.

Years later as a forty-year-old man, L. Frank Baum wove his nightmare of a scarecrow that comes to life into a story he was writing, a sort of "modernized" fairy tale for the new twentieth century. The scarecrow was only one character, though. There was also the Tin Woodman. The idea for that fantasy creature also came from Baum's past, this time from one of his shop window displays. As Harry Baum remembered, his father "wanted to create something eye-catching" for the window of the family's hardware shop in Aberdeen, South Dakota. "So he made a torso out of a wash boiler," Harry explained, "bolted

Title page from *The Wonderful Wizard of Oz*
published in 1900 by the George M. Hill Co.

7

stovepipe arms and legs to it, and used the underside of a saucepan for a face. He topped it with a funnel hat."[1]

By comparison, the heroine of Baum's story was a rather ordinary human girl named Dorothy. Baum never revealed her age or the color of her hair or her eyes. She could have been tall or short, fat or thin. She could have been any child at all. But the adventures she and her dog Toto had were extraordinary. They traveled by cyclone to a land both weird and wonderful. One afternoon while trying to come up with a name for this land of his imagination, Baum glanced at the filing cabinet drawers in his home. The drawer marked "O-Z" caught his eye. Those letters seemed to make as good a name as any for a land peopled with munchkins in the East, flying monkeys in the West, and good witches and bad witches in the North and South.

But the story's mysterious wizard, Oz the Great and Terrible, was Baum's cleverest creation. As a wizard, Oz the Great and Terrible could change shape. Sometimes he appeared as a giant head floating in mid-air. Sometimes he was a great ball of flame. Other times he took the shape of a winged lady. The wizard lived in the Emerald City, a place he himself had built. No one could enter without first locking a pair of green spectacles over their eyes. The glasses were for protection, the Guardian of the Gate explained to Dorothy when she showed up one day with Toto and her friends—the Scarecrow, the Tin Man, and the Cowardly Lion.

"If you did not wear the spectacles," the Guardian warned them, "the brightness and glory of the Emerald City would blind you. Even those who live in the City must wear spectacles, night and day. They are all locked on, for Oz so ordained it when the city was first built, and I have the only key that will unlock them."

As Dorothy eventually discovered, Oz the Great and Terrible was not what he at first appeared to be. He wasn't a wizard at all. He was just an old man from Omaha, Nebraska, with a bald head and wrinkles.

With smoke and mirrors, wires and ventriloquism— and yes, even those amazing green spectacles, which made the Emerald City seem to glow with real jewels—he created his illusions. But when he was found out, the old man confessed, "I have been making believe."

This book of stories is about wizards—wizards of the media. Like Oz the Great and Terrible, these real-life image- makers use smoke and mirrors to con- struct thousands of messages each day. Of course it isn't necessary to travel to a faraway land to experience these messages.

They're off to see the wizard: L. Frank Baum's characters Scarecrow, Tin Man, Dorothy, and Cowardly Lion came to life on the silver screen in the 1939 film *The Wizard of Oz*.

They appear everywhere, on television and radio, in newspapers, magazines, and movie theaters, on billboards and buses, T-shirts and sneakers. Like Oz, too, many of these wizards are "making believe." Some news stories that first appear to be factual turn out to be fabrications. A movie that seems to retell history is just a wizard's interpretation of what *might have happened*. Some advertisements that make factual claims are obviously false.

Media wizards are a creative bunch. They produce their messages using a warehouse of tools—visual effects, sound effects, words that have positive or negative connotations, headlines that SCREAM! and photographs that sensationalize. Some wizards speak in sound bites and advertising slogans. Others mouth media metaphors. But their words and their illusions aren't magic. They are simply messages, each constructed with a purpose—to inform, to persuade, to sell, or influence behavior.

The stories in this book pull back the curtain to reveal the image-makers at work. Are you ready to unlock your green spectacles? Good.

Then we're off
to see the
wizard...or
rather, the
wizards.

Part One

THE WIZARD'S LANGUAGE

Learning the Media Code Words

Can you tell the difference between what's **fact** and what's fiction in the news stories you read? The photographs you see? The movies you watch? Very likely the media wizards have fooled you more than once. That's because the media has a whole vocabulary of "code words" that they understand but that other people may not.

Here's an example. In 1863 during the American Civil War, Colonel Robert Gould Shaw died while leading his men in an attack on Fort Wagner in North Carolina. His men were Negroes, soldiers in the 54th Massachusetts Volunteer Regiment. In 1989 screenwriter Kevin Jarre told the story of the 54th in the award-winning film *Glory*. In writing his version of the story, however, Jarre took some liberties with the facts. The characters of Tripp and Rawlins, played by actors Denzel Washington and Morgan Freeman, weren't real people. They were composites.

A composite is a single fictional character or event based on the combined characteristics of several real people or events. While Tripp and Rawlins might not have lived, people like them certainly did. Jarre created the composites in order to build a suspenseful plot and add symbolism and meaning to his story. According to historian James McPherson, the only character in *Glory* who wasn't a composite was Colonel Shaw. Jarre did not stray from the facts in presenting Colonel Shaw's screen character.

"Composite" is a **media code word** that image-makers understand and use often, especially in fiction writing. In nonfiction writing like newspaper and magazine articles, however, composites must be clearly identified as being "made up" or the writer risks losing his or her job for deceiving the public. Guess what? Sometimes they don't fess up, and even their editors and publishers can be fooled.

"Some of us believe everything we see and read. And some of us believe nothing," says Michael Gartner, publisher of *The Daily Tribune* in Ames, Iowa. "Unless we know the code, we can't be sure what is fact and what is fiction."

The first step in revealing how the media wizards work, therefore, is learning their language. That's what the stories in this section are all about.

By Matthew Lewis—The Washington Post

The Washington Post   September 28, 1980

JIMMY'S WORLD

8-Year-Old Heroin Addict Lives for a Fix

By Janet Cooke
Washington Post Staff Writer

THE 1981
PULITZER PRIZE
FOR FEATURE WRITING
JANET COOKE
THE WASHINGTON POST

The Washington Post

JIMMY'S WORLD

Crossing the Line From Fact to Fiction

He was eight years old and except for the needle marks on his thin brown arm, he looked like most boys. He played baseball. He wore designer sneakers. His name was Jimmy and, according to a feature news story that appeared in the Sunday, September 28, 1980, edition of *The Washington Post*, he was a heroin addict. Janet Cooke, the author of the piece, suggested to the reader that she had been present and actually witnessed Jimmy's mother's boyfriend inserting a heroin-filled needle into Jimmy's arm. Cooke wrote:

> [He] *grabs Jimmy's left arm just above the elbow, his massive hand tightly encircling the child's small limb. The needle slides into the boy's soft skin like a straw pushed into the center of a freshly baked cake. Liquid ebbs out of the syringe, replaced by bright red blood. The blood is then re-injected into the child.*[2]

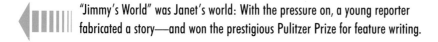

"Jimmy's World" was Janet's world: With the pressure on, a young reporter fabricated a story—and won the prestigious Pulitzer Prize for feature writing.

Janet Cooke's words wowed her editors who nominated the story for a Pulitzer Prize. Equally wowed, the judging committee selected Cooke's story to receive journalism's highest award for 1981. "Jimmy's World" was a far, far cry from Dorothy and Toto's adventures in *The Wizard of Oz*. And yet, the two stories share one thing in common: They are both fiction.

> In newspaper lingo, fabricating a story is called piping. Even though it has a term, piping is not acceptable.

In the days following the announcement that Janet Cooke had won a Pulitzer Prize, the managing editors of *The Washington Post* discovered in alarm that Jimmy did not live in Southeast Washington, D.C. He resided solely in Janet Cooke's imagination. In a tearful 2:00 A.M. confrontation with her bosses at the *Post*, Cooke admitted, "There is no Jimmy." She had made up the story.

By 7:00 A.M., Cooke's resignation was official and the *Post* notified the Pulitzer Prize committee that they were returning the prize. Cooke's boss, Ben Bradlee, offered to resign as well. But that didn't happen. Cooke slipped quietly away into anonymity. The story of her deception had made headlines of its own. No respectable newspaper would hire her.

Many years later, in June 1994, *Time* magazine ran on its cover a photograph of O. J. Simpson taken by police the day they charged him with the murder of his former wife, Nicole Brown Simpson, and her friend, Ronald Goldman. The magazine's designer altered the police mug shot, darkening it for drama. *Time*'s alteration differs from Janet Cooke's fabrication in one way: The *Time* editors told their readers that they had doctored the photograph for effect, but they told them in

A mug of O.J.: A blank canvas for *Time* magazine's editors, who doctored the shot and called it a "photo illustration."

code. In small type on the table of contents page, they identified the cover image as a *photo-illustration*. Photo-illustration is another code word in the language of the media wizards.

The codes aren't limited to just newspapers and news magazines. *Jenny*, a popular television talk show of the 1990s, invited a guest to appear on the program under specific premises, perhaps to share a personal story of overcoming a failed romance or coping with the loss of a child. Then Jenny confronted the guest with an unexpected turn of events—a person from the past, a secret admirer, or a revelation about something personal in the guest's life. The hoped-for effect was shock, or, at the minimum, surprise. The technique was common on many television talk shows, and it, too, had a code word—*ambushing*.

Filmmaker Oliver Stone made a fictional movie, *JFK*, about the conspiracy theories surrounding the assassination of President John F. Kennedy. Stone *framed* the opening scenes with actual black-and-white newsreel footage of the president and Mrs. Kennedy arriving at the Dallas, Texas, airport on the morning of the president's assassination, November 22, 1963. Later in the film, Stone used another media code,

A photo-illustration is any photograph that an image-maker alters in some way, such as darkening or coloring the image, erasing blemishes or background details, or adding details that were not part of the original image.

17

A movie's 𝖿𝗋𝖺𝗆𝖾 helps to set the time and place of the story. By using black-and-white newsreels, Stone sent a message to his viewers that *JFK* was about a real event in history.

montage, to depict a cover-up during the autopsy of the dead president. Even though most of the movie was shot in color, Stone filmed the fictional autopsy montage in black and white.

Even the use of black-and-white film is a code. It is a visual language that creates a particular effect. Was Oliver Stone purposely trying to confuse the viewer into thinking the autopsy was as real as the

A 𝗆𝗈𝗇𝗍𝖺𝗀𝖾 is a series of short scenes or images on film. When viewed one after the other, the individual scenes create a single message or implied meaning. A common use of montage is to show the passage of time or a change in a person or place during a period of time. Image-makers also use montage to create suspense or mystery.

news clips of Kennedy's motorcade through Dallas? Perhaps. Stone created the image, then left its interpretation up to the viewer.

Image-makers—whether they are writers, photographers, talk-show producers and hosts, or filmmakers—use a variety of construction techniques in creating their media messages. They do so in order to sell a product or entertain or influence their audiences.

"Photographers have been touching up photos forever," says newspaper publisher Michael Gartner. "They take out the blemishes and iron out the wrinkles. Reporters have been scrubbing up quotes forever. They take out the 'ums' and 'ers' and tidy up grammar. But somewhere," warns Gartner, "there's a line you do not cross."

Gartner ought to know. He was president of NBC Television News in the early 1990s when reporters working on a *Dateline* story "crossed the line." The story, reported in 1993, was an investigation into a particular make of General Motors (GM) truck with a sidesaddle gas tank that, when involved in a side impact crash, exploded. In constructing the story, the image-makers decided they wanted to show a truck actually crashing, then exploding. To do that, they had to create a crash scene. Their first attempt involved rolling a car down a hill into the truck. The first crash started a small fire, but nothing very alarming. The second crash resulted in no fire at all. Without a blaze, the *Dateline* reporters didn't have a very exciting story to report. And so the image-makers went to work. They replaced the properly fitting gas cap with one that didn't fit and so popped off during impact. Under the rear fender, they rigged a "toy rocket" that exploded, igniting the gas that had spilled from the tank. At last, they had their explosion. Even then, they edited the film footage from the crash, using a *tight shot*. In this case, the tight shot made the fire seem larger. When it aired on *Dateline*, the truck looked as if it were "engulfed in flames."[3]

Dateline crossed the line. If the producers had told their viewers about the special props and camera angle they used and why—to create more dramatic, frightening film footage, GM might not have sued NBC News. But *Dateline* didn't, and GM did. Michael Gartner said he

A **tight shot** is a camera angle that provides a close-up of a subject, focusing not on the whole but on a specific point or part. Image-makers often use tight shots for emphasis or drama.

knew nothing of the rigged demonstration. Even so, as the president of NBC News, he was the man in charge. He voluntarily resigned and headed off to Ames, Iowa.

Janet Cooke was a young reporter, just twenty-six years old and on the job at *The Washington Post* less than year when she won and lost her Pulitzer Prize for a nonfiction story that was really fiction. Surely there were and still are children like Jimmy, addicted to heroin. Sadly, just as Cooke's story suggested, many become addicted through abusive adults. Jimmy could have been a composite character, but Cooke never identified him as one. She could have searched longer, harder for a real Jimmy, but she didn't.

"What I did was wrong," Cooke admitted in an interview fifteen years later to a former friend and fellow *Washington Post* writer, Mike Sager. At the time, she was working part-time in a department store. "I regret that I did it…. I'm ashamed that I did it."

The question remains, then, *why* did she do it? Why do any of the media wizards cross the line from fact to fiction?

The answer may have something to do with a warning given to Cooke by her *Washington Post* editor , a no-nonsense newspaper woman. According to Mike Sager, the editor "doled out praise as often as she did harsh criticism."

Over lunch one day, she told Cooke: "You need to remember two things. First, no matter how good your last story was, people around here want to know, 'What are you going to do for me today?' Second, no matter how good a writer you think you are, you're nothing without me. I've made you what you are, honey pie. I can unmake you just as fast."[4]

It was an important lesson in media wizardry. Competition is stiff. If you slip up, you're out. Under tremendous pressure by her editor to come up with a dynamite story within a given deadline, Janet Cooke did the next best thing she could: She invented Jimmy's World.

MEDIA'S LITTLE WHITE LIES

Sound Bites and Bias

"Pa, I cannot tell a lie," the boy confessed to his father. "It was I who did it with my hatchet!"

No document exists to prove that George Washington hacked down a cherry tree, was caught in the act, and confessed. In fact, historians know very little about George's father except that he died when the boy was still young. Nevertheless, writer Parson Weems seeded the story way back in 1818 when he published the first-ever biography of George Washington. The first president of the United States had been dead for nearly twenty years, and so Weems could not have heard the story from him. Weems was on a mission, though. He wanted to prove that the "Father of our Country" was not only a great military leader and president but also a great child inspired by a wise and loving father. And so he invented the story plus a few others, like this one (also taken from Washington's biography):

One day George's father went into the garden, and prepared a little bed of finely pulverized earth, on which he

Washington couldn't, but Weems could—tell a lie, that is, or at least make up a story.

wrote George's name at full, in large letters—then strewing in plenty of cabbage seed, he covered them up, and smoothed all over nicely with the roller.… Not many mornings had passed away before in came George, with eyes wild rolling, and his little cheeks ready to burst with great news. "O, Pa! come here! come here!"

. . . The old gentleman suspecting what George would be at, gave him his hand, which he seized with great eagerness, and tugging him along through the garden, led him point blank to the bed whereon was inscribed in large letters and in all the freshness of newly sprung plants, the full name of GEORGE WASHINGTON.[5]

It's a cute story, but it never happened. Weems slanted his biography to show only the best side of George—as an innocent boy, decisive general, and respected president. That's biased writing.

How do writers create bias? In the case of Parson Weems, they may invent dialogue or imagine entire scenes that fit their intended message or effect. Hence, the infamous cherry tree and the cabbage patch. Or they may select only certain details to include in a story, casting aside the factual information that contradicts their particular image or their intended message.

Bias is an opinion or prejudice, either favorable or unfavorable. Writers use biased writing to influence the opinions or attitudes of others.

Missing from Weems's biography, for example, are some gritty and very human truths about his subject. When the Continental Congress first asked Washington to command the Continental army, the general accepted with valor, but in a private letter to his wife, Martha, he confessed his doubts. To command the entire army was a trust too great for his abilities, he wrote. What if he should fail? By December 1776 the general's private fears had come true. His army was in shambles. The British had soundly defeated them at almost every turn. Except for perhaps a thousand military, the men of the thirteen colonies were refusing to fight under Washington's command. Even his own officers whispered about replacing him. Then, just when he needed it most, he defeated the Hessian soldiers camped at Trenton, New Jersey, in a surprise attack on Christmas morning, 1776. Rumors of replacing the general quieted down, even though the war was far from being won.

But Parson Weems doesn't tell *that* story about Washington. Instead of an image of a complicated man struggling with his own self-doubts and his love of freedom, Weems gave his readers a biased biography that portrays the father of our country as a man who could do no wrong, who was too good to be true. The American reading public of the nineteenth century bought it. Weems's story influenced generations of readers so that today the fictional cherry tree, the cabbage patch, and Washington's good-boy behavior are now firmly rooted in American mythology.

Inventing a false story or slanting a story through the careful selection of details are just two ways a media wizard creates bias. A third way is through the use of *sound bites*. During the 1996 presidential campaign, Bill Clinton addressed the Democratic National Convention for more than an hour, discussing his vision for the future. He talked about education, technology, and the welfare of American citizens. The news media extracted a catchy phrase from that long, detailed speech: *"A bridge to the twenty-first century."* News commentators and reporters and even the candidate himself repeated the phrase over and over. It became the sound bite of Clinton's reelection campaign.

A sound bite is a short extract from a recorded interview, speech, or some other form of communication.

The sound bite is not an invention of the 1990s. It actually began back in radio days, long before television changed the ways Americans viewed and voted for their presidents. In radio, a sound bite was a tape of someone speaking other than the news commentator. It was radio's way of allowing the news *maker* to speak for himself or herself. Then sound bites ran for minutes and could be as long as paragraphs.

Today, a sound bite is still someone speaking on tape or film. The difference is that today, the sound bite is short—and getting shorter every year. In 1968 a typical sound bite from a presidential election was more than forty seconds. In 1996 the sound bite had shriveled to less than ten seconds. Instead of paragraphs, the sound bite is now a single sentence or even a phrase, such as Bill Clinton's *"A bridge to the twenty-first century."* The wizards of the news media also love sound bites—they make great headlines and teasers to get readers to buy a newspaper or stay tuned to a particular television program.

Sound bites reduce complex ideas into catchy phrases. That's where the bias, or prejudice, begins. When people hear or read a sound bite, they aren't hearing or reading the entire message and so the original meaning may be lost or misinterpreted. The result is the same as Parson Weems deleting important details about Washington's inner struggles while the general led his country through a bloody revolution. Because sound bites are repeated *out of context*, they also slant reality.

It take a village to raise a child is an African proverb meaning that a child is loved and cared for not only by his or her parents but also by the community in which the child lives. Working together, the family and the community ensure the rearing of a healthy, happy individual. In 1996, First Lady Hillary Rodham Clinton selected the proverb as the title of her book on children. A few months later the phrase *"It takes a village"* surfaced at the Republican National Convention—this time as a sound bite.

"It doesn't take a village; it takes a family to raise a child," stated Republican presidential candidate Bob Dole. He offered his interpretation of the phrase: The wife of his Democratic opponent believed that the responsibility of rearing and caring for a child belonged not with the family but with the government. The sound bite *"It takes a village"* took on a negative connotation—that parents were shirking their responsibility for rearing their children. Dole took the phrase out

The First Lady was bitten by a proverb-turned-sound bite.

of its original context, choosing not to mention the African proverb from which it had originated. Like Parson Weems, he cast aside the information that didn't fit his message or intended effect.

Of course, bias is not just about dead presidents. Nor does it surface only during presidential election campaigns. Television producers and newspaper editors make biased decisions every day just by deciding which stories to cover and which people to quote. Left on the cutting room floor are the stories and people the media wizards have cast aside. They make these decisions not necessarily because they want to slant reality but because very often there just isn't enough room in the newspaper or enough time during the broadcast to tell the *whole* story. That's the fourth way wizards create bias—through the editing of stories.

In defense of his fellow journalists, ABC television news commentator Peter Jennings argues that bias is a two-way street. Yes, writers may bias their stories intentionally—by inventing or selecting details to fit a predetermined message, by reducing information into ten-second sound bites, or by editing stories to fit a particular media format. But the reader or viewer also plays an important role in the creation of bias. "Try to understand one thing about bias," says Jennings. "It is in the eye of the beholder…. Viewers bring their own personal, social, cultural, racial, political, and economic baggage to the story."[6]

That baggage is often in the form of biased thinking. Readers and viewers have a responsibility to look beyond the slant or sound bite and interpret a story's meaning. But people interpret media messages differently, based on their own experiences or preconceived ideas and prejudices. And that's the fifth way bias enters the media—not only through the words or images of the media wizards but through the eyes and ears of the audience.

AFTER THE BATTLE

Photojournalism at Gettysburg

Rain had fallen on and off for two days. On the morning of July 5 mists still shrouded the fields at Gettysburg, Pennsylvania. A wagon rattled over the field, then stopped. Alexander Gardner stepped down. To his right was Culp's Hill. To his left was Round Top and the forest. What lay before him, scattered thickly throughout the field, was the debris of battle: ammunition, cups, canteens, shattered caissons, and, of course, corpses—human and animal. Gardner took from his wagon his photographic equipment and, joining a burial party, moved among the dead and dying.

Alexander Gardner was one of approximately twenty photographers hired by master photographer Matthew Brady to document the American Civil War. The United States government allowed Brady's men to travel with Union troops. They arrived in wooden vans, on the sides of which was painted *Brady's Photographic Corps.* The back of the enclosed wagon served as a darkroom where the photographer could develop his film. In 1863 photography was an innovation. Cameras

An unwitting conspirator to media wizardry, a soldier who fell in the Battle of Gettysburg was moved from a field to this rock shelter and dubbed a "Rebel Sharpshooter."

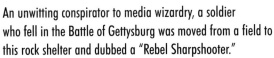

required fifteen-second exposures, so the photographers could not capture the actual fighting. They could only shoot portraits of soldiers in camp or the minutes prior to battle, with men and caissons in position, waiting. Often they arrived after the battle, as Alexander Gardner had at Gettysburg, to record, as Gardner described it, "the blank horror and reality of war."

On that overcast July morning, Gardner shot a number of images. One he titled "A Sharpshooter's Last Sleep." The dead Union soldier was lying on his back. His cap and gun were on the ground behind him. Gardner reasoned that they had been thrown there "by the violence of the shock" that struck and killed the man. Another photograph he titled "The Home of a Rebel Sharpshooter." According to the text Gardner wrote later explaining the image, the Confederate soldier had camped between two boulders. Across the front, he had built a small stone wall. From this sheltered position, he had fired at Union officers. Gardner drew the viewer's attention to white markings on the left boulder, indicating that Union sharpshooters had fired repeatedly into the lair to dislodge the sniper.

The images from Brady's Photographic Corps shocked the country because they were so vivid and gruesome. In 1865, Gardner published a book showcasing these Civil War images. "Here are the dreadful details!" he wrote of his images. "Let them aid in preventing such another calamity falling upon the nation."

Photographs like Gardner's seem to capture moments of truth. During the fifteen-second exposure, the camera lens makes no decisions, no changes. It has no opinion of the objects in its angle of vision; it simply reproduces them on film as they are in reality.

And yet, photographs are also constructed media messages. Many years after Alexander Gardner photographed the unburied bodies at Gettysburg, historians who studied his images have concluded that at times Gardner rearranged the elements in his photographs so their effect was even more dreadful, more horrible. He did so for the very

The **composition** of a photograph is the arrangement of the elements in the picture. Those elements can be people, objects, and settings. Other elements are lighting, camera angles, and use of symbols. Words or captions that accompany the photograph—whether written by the photographer or by an editor—also help to shape the image's effect.

reason he stated in his book—to convince the American public to never again commit such carnage. The dead soldiers in "A Sharpshooter's Last Sleep" and "The Home of a Rebel Sharpshooter" are, in fact, the same man. Historian William Frassanito explains that geographic details place both photographs in the same area, on the southern slope of Devil's Den. According to Frassanito, Gardner first photographed the dead man lying on his back, his hat and gun behind him. Then, using a field blanket, Gardner dragged the corpse to the "picturesque" rock den forty yards away. He arranged the body between the rocks, with the face turned toward the camera.

The dead soldier was not a sharpshooter at all. The rifle above the man's head was not, says Frassanito, the type of weapon used by sharpshooters. Most likely the rifle was Gardner's prop, an object he used in a number of photographs when he felt it was needed.

Gardner claimed that he returned to the Gettysburg battlefield four months later to attend the dedication of the Gettysburg Cemetery. He heard President Lincoln deliver his Gettysburg Address. Then, walking across the hallowed ground, he found again the sharpshooter's den. Gardner wrote of what he saw:

The musket, rusted by many storms, still leaned against the
rock, and the skeleton of the soldier lay undisturbed within
the moldering uniform, as did the cold form of the dead
four months before. None of those who went up and down
the fields to bury the fallen, had found him.

That, too, was a constructed message, one Gardner wrote to ac-company the photograph in his book. Frassanito doubts that the body would have remained unburied and that the rifle would have escaped "the hordes of relic hunters who swarmed over battlefields."

Two other photographs taken at Gettysburg are also not quite what the photograph made them out to be. "A Harvest of Death" and "Field Where General Reynolds Fell" are of the same scene, taken from two different angles by photographer Timothy O'Sullivan. O'Sullivan, like Gardner, was one of Brady's Photographic Corps. The Library of Congress, where the photographs are on file, calls this pair of images "The Case of Confused Identity." Gardner included the pair in his book and wrote text to accompany these images as well as his own. According to Gardner, the corpses in "A Harvest of Death" are Confederate soldiers who have paid with their lives for their treason to the nation. Their shoes have been removed because, as Gardner accurately explains, they were needed by the living.

 Cool trivia: The phrase "biting the bullet" actually comes from the practice of clenching a cartridge of gunpowder in between the teeth while loading the rifle.

Gardner identifies the bodies in the other photograph, "Field Where General Reynolds Fell," as Union soldiers. The faces of some were frozen in their final agony. Many more though, he wrote,

had a smile on their faces, and looked as if they were in the
act of speaking. Some lay stretched on their backs, as if

Traitorous rebels or valiant heroes? You decide. "A Harvest of Death," (above) and "Field Where General Reynolds Fell" (below) show the same soldiers photographed from different directions and angles but described in very different terms.

friendly hands had prepared them for burial. Some were still resting on one knee, their hands grasping their muskets. In some instances the cartridge remained between the teeth....The faces of all were pale, as though cut in marble, and as the wind swept across the battlefield it waved the hair, and gave the bodies such an appearance of life that a spectator could hardly help thinking they were about to rise to continue the fight.[7]

In both photographs a diamond badge is visible on the uniform of one of the dead soldiers. Union III Corps soldiers wore such a badge. Confederate soldiers did not. The contortions of the bodies—an outstretched arm, a bent knee—are evidence also that the corpses are the same Union soldiers in both photographs. O'Sullivan had shot the bodies from opposite angles.

The photographs of Alexander Gardner and Timothy O'Sullivan are striking. They remain an important piece of American history. But questions remain: Why move a corpse from one location to another? Why add a prop to the composition? Why shoot a scene from two different angles and then falsely identify the corpses in one image as Union soldiers and those in the other as Confederate soldiers? Why, also, write text that describes the Confederate soldiers as traitors and the Union soldiers as heroes about to wake and fight again?

The answer lies in the individual photographer's purpose and intended effect. Alexander Gardner, for example, was loyal to the Union. He did not wear a uniform, but if he had it would have been blue, not gray. His purpose was to document a war. But it was also to stir patriotism in Americans and, above all else, to reveal in harsh detail the tragedy of that war. At times the best way to achieve that effect was to rearrange the elements in the composition of his photographs.

THE METAPHOR IS THE MESSAGE

Using Symbolism in a Public Service Announcement

The room is dark, enclosed, and windowless. In the center is a swimming pool. The water steams and glows an eerie green. Strangely clad creatures—humans in environmental protection suits that cover them from head to toe—pour a thick tar into the stewing pool. Suddenly, an alarm buzzes. It sounds again and again in sync with a flashing yellow light. From somewhere beyond the pool area a voice over a loudspeaker states calmly, "Thirty seconds. Please transfer immediately." Obediently, the hooded creatures file from the area, passing through doors that seal tightly behind them.

Is this a scene from a science-fiction television series—perhaps *Star Trek* or *Deep Space Nine*? Is it a teaser for a soon-to-be-released fantasy movie?

It is neither. It is a public service announcement (PSA) called "Swimmers" created for the Ontario Ministry of Health in Canada by the advertising firm Vickers & Benson. Most PSAs are ten or thirty seconds in length. But "Swimmers" is a ninety-second spot, a *media metaphor* with a stunning, hard-hitting antismoking message. As the film continues, three swimmers enter the now-cleared pool area. They are teenagers—a boy and two girls. They each wear a white swimming suit. Barefoot, they move along a gangway to the edge of the pool. Above them, on the other side of a glass window, adults wearing white laboratory coats watch with anticipation.

"Rocket fuel, arsenic, toilet bowl cleaner, cyanide, paint remover, ant poison…are waiting for you," a voice-over is speaking. One girl turns her back to the pool, bends her knees, and arches into a backdive. "Take up cigarette smoking if you want to," the voice tells the swimmers, "just know what you're getting into." The second girl dives and then, at last, the boy, too, leaps. A message appears across the screen: SMOKING—IT'LL SUCK THE LIFE RIGHT OUT OF YOU.

The process involved in creating "Swimmers" involved a number of creative media wizards at Vickers & Benson. The Ontario Ministry of Health wanted the PSA to be a persuasive message about the dan-

A metaphor is an implied comparison between two things that are unrelated. When poet Carl Sandburg wrote: *"The fog comes on little cat feet,"* he was comparing fog to a cat. Although fog and cats are significantly different, they share one thing in common—the silent way of sneaking up on a person. A media metaphor is also an implied comparison. Whereas literary metaphors use only words, media metaphors blend words and visual images—and sometimes even sound effects—to suggest a shared characteristic between two otherwise different things.

gers of smoking. The creative team's first step was to learn as much as they could about their target audience—children—and the reasons they smoke. To help them, they hired a cultural anthropologist.

An anthropologist is a person who studies humans—what they like, dislike, fear, and desire. Here is what the creative team at Vickers & Benson learned about children from the anthropologist:

- *Most children begin to experiment with cigarettes by age ten. That meant that if the Ministry of Health's PSA was to be effective, it needed to appeal to preteens.*

- *Most ten- and eleven-year-old children can't wait to become teenagers. That suggested to the team that the "swimmers" in the PSA should be older than the target audience of preteens.*

- *Peer pressure is an important influence on children, but it isn't the only reason they begin or continue to smoke. "One of our most fundamental discoveries in this [research] process was that smoking isn't simple," said Dave Snell, a vice president at Vickers & Benson. "You can't just say, 'Oh, it's just peer pressure. Oh, it's just rebellion.' It's a very complex behavior." Because the pressure to smoke is so complicated, the creative team at Vickers & Benson realized their PSA message couldn't be "Just say no." Somehow, they had to develop a message with a stronger emotional punch.*

- *Many children are concerned about chemicals that pollute the environment. That bit of information sparked the creative idea for the PSA. Rolled into a single cigarette are thousands of chemicals, like arsenic and nicotine. Right away the team knew they wanted to make a link between the chemicals in cigarettes and a poisoned environment. The way to do it was through a media metaphor.*

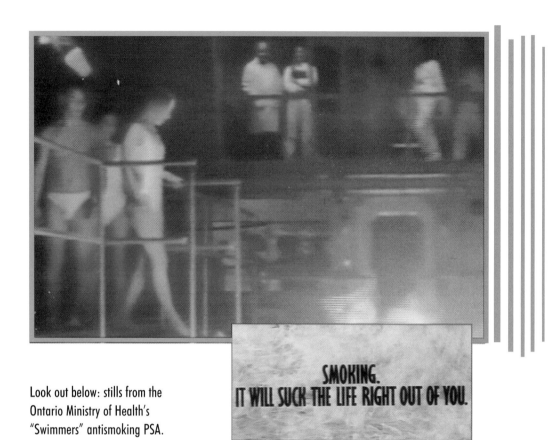

SMOKING.
IT WILL SUCK THE LIFE RIGHT OUT OF YOU.

Look out below: stills from the Ontario Ministry of Health's "Swimmers" antismoking PSA.

Now that they had a concept and their toxic swimming pool metaphor, the team moved into the storyboard stage. A storyboard is like a cartoon. Each frame on the board depicts a scene or key event in the film or movie. Attention to detail is very important. Frame by frame, the team sketches the characters, the costumes, the setting, and even lines of dialogue, using media codes to construct the metaphor and the message. The humans encased in environmental protection suits are a visual code suggesting contamination. The buzzing alarm and the flashing yellow light are sound codes signaling danger. Even the color of the swimmers' suits was a code—white for innocence or purity.

"Swimmers" ends just as the teenagers disappear beneath the water. What the viewer doesn't see is what happens next.

Do the swimmers emerge from the pool, gasping for breath? Do they climb out of the water, shivering but safe? Does one of the adults in the white lab coats suddenly have a change of heart and rescue the swimmers?

The decision of how to end a film is also part of the media metaphor and its message. By ending the film with the water bubbling and sizzling, the advertising team at Vickers & Benson are saying—metaphorically of course—that the outcome is in the hands of the viewers.

Part Two

ADVERTISING FICTIONS

Advertising and Marketing Wizardry

In the 1930s a psychologist named Louis Cheskin conducted studies to test people's emotional responses to product packaging. He placed the same product in two different packages. On the exterior of the first package were circles. On the exterior of the second package were triangles. Cheskin asked his subjects which product they preferred, but he did not ask them to comment on the package designs. What Cheskin discovered amazed him! Although both packages contained the same product, 80 percent of the people preferred the product in the box with the circles. Cheskin concluded that they had been attracted to the circles and transferred the emotion triggered by the design to the contents inside.

Cheskin called his discovery "sensation transference." Additional studies he conducted showed that colors, too, create certain sensations in people: bright red quickens the pulse; blue calms the nerves. The manufacturers of Tide laundry detergent used Cheskin's findings to design the bright orange bull's-eye logo for their packages.

Bold colors and circles on cardboard boxes are just one way to persuade a consumer to purchase a product. Today, packaging still means presentation, but presentation can include visuals, sound effects, story lines—in short, all kinds of sensations and images. The theory, however, remains the same: Get the consumer to buy into a feel-good image and they'll automatically transfer it to the product.

Welcome to the world of advertising and marketing wizardry.

CAUGHT IN THE PRESS AGENT'S CROSSHAIRS

Targeting an Audience

The Great War had ended and the soldiers were returning home from the battlefields of Europe. Nobody then called it World War I because nobody believed that humans could ever repeat such a terrible slaughter.

Edward L. Bernays had gone to war but not as a combat soldier. Words were his weapons. He worked for the United States' War Department Committee on Public Information (CPI). The CPI's goal was to drum up American patriotism and support for the war effort. Without that support, the government could not recruit a sizable army or raise the money to arm its soldiers. And so the government paid writers like Bernays to pen patriotic newspaper editorials and pamphlets (called "Red, White and Blue" books) to convince the public that the war was just. CPI slogans like "The war to end all wars" and "The war to make the world safe for democracy" were propaganda statements. They stirred the hearts—but not necessarily the minds—of wives and mothers, fathers and sons, calling on them to sacrifice whatever was needed, even their lives, to win the war.

After the war Bernays found new ways to use his powers of persuasion. He became a press agent.

In the 1920s a press agent created publicity for a person or a company and its products or services. "Publicizing" could earn an agent as much as $1,500 a week—an incredible sum! After all, a new Model T Ford cost about $400! Even so, being a press agent wasn't a very respectable profession, in part because the agents frequently used tricks and deception to "create news" on behalf of their clients.

For example, as a gimmick to improve the public's image of businessman John D. Rockefeller, press agent Ivy Lee convinced the billionaire to give away dimes on street corners. Lee made certain the press was present to capture the gentleman's generous gesture.

Press agent Harry Reichenbach boasted about his ability to "plant" false stories in the news. During a New York City court hearing investigating whether Reichenbach had concocted a "stunt suicide" in a Central Park lake to promote a soon-to-be-released movie, Reichenbach denied the charge and called the stunt "crude." However, he did admit to the district attorney that he had "used his wits" to create a fake kidnapping of an American actress by Mexicans. The kidnapping and the rescue of the young lady by eight blond cavalry men was a planned publicity stunt, also for a movie promotion.

"I can't see what harm a good fake does to anybody," Reichenbach added in his own defense.

Propaganda devices are persuasive ways of spreading ideas and influencing behavior, most often by manipulating human desires and fears!

Don't spend it all in one place: John D. Rockefeller hands a dime to his golf caddy. Although it was a publicity stunt, the "Rockefeller Dime" giveaway represented in a small way the philanthropic work he did.

Not only were the Ivory Soap sculpting contests good advertising, they were good, clean fun.

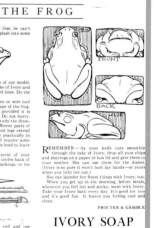

IVORY SOAP

SCULPTURE

LESSON NO. 7   By MARGARET J. POSTGATE

THE FROG

HERE we have Mr. Bullfrog so that he can't possibly hop away and go ker-splash into some brook or pool.

To carve him, we start at the top of our model. Draw his outline carefully on your cake of Ivory and cut away all the soap up to the dotted lines. Do the same with the sides.

Then go to work with your wooden or wire tool and shave or cut down to the real shape of the frog. You will find that your wire tool, provided it is firmly made, is better for this work. Do not hurry. Turn your model often. It is well to study the drawings closely to see just where the different parts of the frog come on your soap. The hind legs extend from the back to the center and are practically in three parts. The eyes bulge and will require some care. Be sure when you are carving his head to leave enough soap to make the eyes.

As the very last step, use the point of your wooden tool to draw in his ears (the circles back of his eyes) his wide mouth; and the markings on his feet.

YOUR TOOLS:

1. Penknife or paring knife
2. Orange stick with one blade end and one pointed end (wooden tool, A)
3. One orange stick with hairpin tied to end and filed sharp (wire tool, B, C, and D)

REMEMBER—As your knife cuts smoothly through the cake of Ivory, drop all your chips and shavings on a paper or box lid and give them to your mother. She can use them for the dishes (Ivory is so pure it won't hurt her hands—or yours when you help her out.)

She can launder her finest things with Ivory, too.

When you get up in the morning, before meals, whenever you feel hot and sticky, wash with Ivory. Take your Ivory bath every day. It's good for you and it's good fun. It leaves you feeling cool and clean.

PROCTER & GAMBLE

IVORY SOAP

99 44/100% Pure   It Floats

© 1926, P. & G. Co.

Edward Bernays was also a master of manipulating the press. In the 1920s, to sell Ivory Soap for its manufacturer, Procter & Gamble, Bernays created the National Soap Sculpture Contest. More than a million people shaved and carved miniature sculptures from the white bars. Bernays called such staged news events *over acts.* "Creating news" in this way, he said, was the press agent's most important task. He was also the first person to use the phrase "public relations" to mean the swaying of public opinion. And he had some very specific ideas about just how to do it.

"The human being—male or female—is a herd animal," he wrote in his 1923 book titled *Crystallizing Public Opinion.* "Man is fearful of solitude.… He is more sensitive to the voice of the herd than to any other influence."

According to Bernays, the goal of the public relations expert is to influence opinion. The way to do that is to create in the individual a desire to be like everybody else. In other words, get them to follow the herd. That is exactly the approach Bernays took when the American Tobacco Company hired him in the late 1920s. The Great War had done great things for cigarette makers. Soldiers who had begun to smoke cigarettes while in the trenches overseas had not given up the habit once they returned home. That was the good news. Most women, however, were not smokers—at least not in public. Society frowned upon women who smoked. They weren't ladies, they were…well, something cheaper than a lady. Because half the population was women—and that was a very large herd indeed—changing society's attitude about women smokers was necessary if cigarette makers were to increase sales and profits.

Bernays went to work. The first step in developing a public relations campaign, he said, was to understand the client's aim. His client was the American Tobacco Company. Their aim was to sell cigarettes to women. The company had even developed a special brand just for women—Marlboros.

The second step in the campaign was to understand the client's target audience. Since the war, women's lives had been changing. In 1919 women suffragists, who for years had marched with linked arms in parades to demand equal rights, had finally won a key victory—the right to vote. More women were now working outside the home, in factories and mills and business offices. A growing number of doctors, lawyers, and scientists were also women. Even those who didn't work, the daughters of socially prominent families, were changing. These debutantes, as they were called, had raised their hemlines and bobbed their hair. Bernays saw all these changes in women as a demand for independence and equal rights. That became the key message in his campaign.

Aim, target, campaign—the code words of public relations used language often reserved for war. Bernays welcomed the battle. On Easter Sunday, 1929, he set out to capture the women of America.

He called cigarettes "torches of freedom." Women had fought for the right to vote and they had won. But they still were not free to smoke in public. Believing that most women, like most men, were herd animals, he created an over act to catch the attention of the public and especially news reporters and photographers. The Easter Parade was a New York City society event. Bernays hired a number of debutantes to march in that parade, dressed in their finest clothing, of course, but also smoking their "torches of freedom."

The women marched. The press pounced, as planned. Photographs and articles about the women's rebellion appeared in newspapers beyond New York City. Bernays had succeeded in showing the "society herd" smoking. Soon, hundreds of thousands of women followed the herd's example. Cigarette sales among women soared.

Of course, Bernays was not the only person working hard to sell smoking to women. A few years earlier, the makers of Chesterfield cigarettes created a billboard advertisement that showed a man and

From "Mild as May" to Macho Man

Marlboro's red "beauty tip," white package, and slogan "Mild as May" lasted until 1954. Decreasing sales to women, however, meant a shift in strategy. The cigarette manufacturer hired a new public relations firm to tackle the problem. The Leo Burnett Agency in Chicago decided to forget women and target men instead. They lost the red tip and gave the package strong red and white colors and a new fliptop. They also created a cowboy image to suggest ruggedness and masculinity. The Marlboro Man roped in a whole new herd of male smokers.

woman sitting together on a beach at night. The man is smoking. The woman says, "Blow some my way." In another advertisement, a woman gazes longingly at a man seated in a chair and smoking a pipe. *"I wish I were a man,"* she thinks.

Not everyone followed the herd. A December 18, 1929, article in the magazine *The Christian Century* called the recent advertising campaign targeting women "disgraceful" and the women portrayed in the advertisements "greasy-haired" Medusas. Even so, the practice of targeting women continued successfully. In the 1930s the manufacturers of Marlboros created a "beauty tip" as a way to appeal to ladies. The red paper on the tip of the cigarette hid lipstick smears and prevented bits of tobacco from sticking to a lady's lips.

"*Light a Lucky* and you'll never miss sweets that make you fat"

Constance Talmadge

Constance Talmadge,
Charming Motion
Picture Star

INSTEAD of eating between meals ... instead of fattening sweets ... beautiful women keep youthful slenderness these days by smoking Luckies. The smartest and loveliest women of the modern stage take this means of keeping slender ... when others nibble fattening sweets, they light a Lucky!

Lucky Strike is a delightful blend of the world's finest tobaccos. These tobaccos are toasted—a costly extra process which develops and improves the flavor. That's why Luckies are a delightful alternative for fattening sweets. That's why there's real health in Lucky Strike. That's why folks say: "It's good to smoke Luckies."

For years this has been no secret to those men who keep fit and trim. They know that Luckies steady their nerves and do not harm their physical condition. They know that Lucky Strike is the favorite cigarette of many prominent athletes, who must keep in good shape. They respect the opinions of 20,679 physicians who maintain that Luckies are less irritating to the throat than other cigarettes.

A reasonable proportion of sugar in the diet is recommended, but the authorities are overwhelming that too many fattening sweets are harmful and that too many such are eaten by the American people. So, for moderation's sake we say:—

"REACH FOR A LUCKY
INSTEAD OF A SWEET."

Constance Talmadge,
Charming Motion
Picture Star

"It's toasted"

No Throat Irritation-No Cough.

Reach for a
Lucky instead
of a sweet

coast to coast radio hook-up every Saturday night through the National Broadcasting

Like the slogans developed by the CPI during World War I, the advertising jingles thought up by press agents were also propaganda messages. *"Reach for a Lucky instead of a sweet…Be happy, go Lucky/ Be happy, Go Lucky Strike today!"* convinced women that smoking was not only a right but also an enjoyable pastime.

For the smokers caught in the press agent's crosshairs, the slogans, the publicity stunts, and the planted news stories were not always, as Harry Reichenbach had suggested, without harm. As early at the 1930s, Edward Bernays had learned that smoking might be linked to cancer. In private, he stole his wife's cigarettes and destroyed them. In public, he continued to create persuasive messages to lure smokers to the product, including the suggestion that smoking would help an overweight person lose weight.

Then in December 1952, *Reader's Digest* published an article that changed everything. "Cancer by the Carton" revealed the results of scientific studies linking smoking to lung cancer. Because of the cancer scare, sales dropped. Once again, the tobacco manufacturers called upon their press agents (now called PR, or public relations, specialists) to sway public opinion. The aim and the target hadn't changed, but the campaign strategy had. A barrage of cigarette advertising hit print venues—magazines, billboards, radio and television. The filter wars had begun.

> *Switch to Juleps and smoke all you want!*
> *A smoking miracle? Yes, and it's the triple miracle of mint.*

The advertisement for Julep's mint filter claimed that the mentholated filter kept the mouth from getting "smoke-weary," prevented that "dry-as-dust rawness" and "harsh, hacking feeling" in the throat. As an added health benefit, it freshened breath.

The PR team for Viceroy cigarettes pitched their healthy smoking message to doctors. One advertisement placed in medical journals

 A 1929 Lucky Strike cigarette ad—fat was probably the least of her worries.

claimed: *"Doctor, when your patients ask… What have Viceroys got that other filter tip cigarettes haven't got? The answer is 200,000 filters in every Viceroy tip."* Another advertisement claimed: *"Nurses everywhere are discussing these important differences in Viceroy's filter tip."*

The advertising claims of the 1950s about the miracle of mint and 200,000 filters in a single cigarette tip were no different from Bernays's "torches of freedom," Ivy Lee's Rockefeller dime giveaway gimmick, or Harry Reichenbach's phony kidnappings. They were all strategies in campaigns created purposely to sway public opinion.

Public relations strategies haven't changed very much since the days following the Great War. Companies still hire press agents to create over acts for their products. They still follow Bernays's advice to know the client's aim. As Bernays discovered while working for the CPI, words and images can indeed be weapons. As long as there is a product to sell, whether it is a movie, soap, or a brand of cigarette, there will always be someone in the press agent's crosshairs.

HERE COMES SANTA CLAUS

How Copywriters and Marketers Celebrate the Holidays

In the nineteenth century, two things occurred that forever changed holiday gift giving. First, the industrialization of the nation introduced mass production. Machines could make toys—and just about everything else—faster and more cheaply than people could make them by hand.

Second, two writers, Washington Irving and Dr. Clement Clarke Moore, both wrote about a peddler who gave gifts at Christmas to children who were nice, not naughty. Irving published his story of Saint Nicholas in 1809. The old man in his story traveled by horse and wagon and tossed toys for good children down chimneys. A few years later in 1823, Moore published his poem "A Visit From Saint Nicholas." Gone were the horse and wagon. In their place was a sleigh and eight reindeer. The legend of the American Santa was born.

Many more years passed, however, before cartoonist Thomas Nast decided one day to illustrate the details of Moore's poem. He

published his image of Saint Nicholas as a jolly old fellow with a white beard in magazines and newspapers across the country. Large department stores at this time were exciting, innovative places to shop. The store owners saw a marketing opportunity in Nash's drawings and in the make-believe story overall. Forget visions of sugarplums! Those stockings hanging by the chimney could be stuffed with mass-produced, store-bought toys instead of sweets. In the 1870s, Macy's department store in New York City launched the first-ever campaign to encourage the buying of gifts from a store for Christmas.

Other large department stores such as Gimbel's in Philadelphia and Hudson's in Detroit also began promoting the holidays. In 1920, Gimbel's organized the first-ever Thanksgiving Day parade, with Santa Claus as the celebrated guest. A few years later, Macy's imitated the idea and sponsored its own Thanksgiving parade. To increase profits even more, Fred Lazarus, Jr., founder of the Federated Department Stores in Ohio, persuaded President Franklin D. Roosevelt in 1941 to change the day on which Thanksgiving fell to add six more shopping days to the Christmas season.

Today, holiday promotions begin in October, run through Super Bowl Sunday in late January, and include a growing list of celebrations: Halloween, Thanksgiving, Kwanzaa, Hanukkah, Christmas, and New Year's Day. During that three-month shopping spree, Americans spend more than $80 billion on holiday-related purchases, and retail stores and toy manufacturers earn as much as 50 percent of their yearly profits.

That kind of spending and profiting is not an accident. It is the result of carefully constructed strategies. Behind each store display for monster masks and pumpkin-colored candy, behind each thirty-second TV spot for Nintendo 64 and Christmas Barbie, behind each catalogue mailed from the over-the-rainbow lands of L. L. Bean and J. Crew is a team of professional marketing wizards known as *copywriters* and *marketers*.

Thomas Nast introduced this rendition of jolly old St. Nick in the 1860s, and it stuck.

Copywriters begin with a choice. Most advertisements can be classified into one of two types: Ads that focus on the product's benefits, and ads that focus on image. Or, as the *Journal of Advertising* puts it, *thinking* ads and *feeling* ads.

Although the purpose of both thinking and feeling ads is the same—to influence behavior—the ads differ in their message strategies. When creating a thinking ad, the copywriter focuses on the product: What are its benefits? What makes it unique? When creating a feeling ad, the copywriter focuses on the users of the products: What needs or wants do they have? What images will get their attention and influence them to buy?

Copywriters write the words and conceive the images for print and video campaigns, which put the product and its advertising before the public. **Marketers,** on the other hand, develop strategies to reach the target audience. They decide where and when the copywriters' advertisements will appear.

During the holidays, feeling ads dominate the airwaves and the printed page. Copywriters working for Folger's coffee created a sentimental thirty-second spot about a son returning home on leave from the military. He arrives early on Christmas morning and awakens the family, and the viewer's emotions too, by brewing a fresh pot of coffee. Copywriters working for Hershey came up with a different "feeling" concept to sell chocolate. A father and son are on a snowy sleigh ride. The horse-drawn carriage journeys to a cottage called "Hershey's Pot of Gold." This is, in the copywriter's words, "a place where choco-

One of Santa's helpers auctions off a Tickle Me Elmo doll in 1996. After it went for $155, maybe it should have been called "Tackle My Wallet."

late is everything." When the camera pulls back, the viewer sees that the father and son are living—magically—inside a snow globe.

Once the copywriter creates the advertisement, the marketers take over. Their job is to determine the best placement for the advertisement. If it is a television commercial, will it be more effective if aired on a Sunday evening or a Saturday morning? If it is print advertising, in which magazines or newspapers should it appear? The answer depends on who is watching television when and who is reading which magazines.

There is another way to place a product: Get someone on television to endorse it. That's just what the marketers working for the Tyco toy company did one holiday season. Tyco had a new kiddie toy, a furry little red fellow called Tickle Me Elmo. When squeezed, the stuffed toy wiggled and laughed. Sales were slow. Then the marketers got a brainstorm. They shipped Elmos to television talk-show hosts across the country. When Rosie O'Donnell featured the toy on her popular daytime show, she triggered what the media later dubbed "Elmomania." Suddenly, everybody had to have an Elmo. Frantic parents called store after store searching for Elmo. Some parents ran alongside delivery trucks. Others ripped Elmos from one another's hands at the checkout counter.

So much for holiday cheer.

In ancient Rome the emperor Caligula passed a law forcing his subjects to present him with New Year's gifts. He stood on the palace steps awaiting his bounty. Beware the citizen who didn't hand over something. In present-day America, no law requires parents or children to buy gifts for the holidays. Still, as long as there are consumers, there will also be copywriters and marketers developing new strategies to sell them all sorts of sugarplums.

Santa Claus has come to town—and moved in for good.

FIVE WAYS TO WANT

Recognizing Advertising Subtexts

A man wearing a tuxedo dives from an airplane just minutes before it explodes. No, it isn't a scene from a James Bond movie. It is a commercial for a citrus soft drink that's high in caffeine and daredeviltry. In 1996 thirsty people around the world, mostly between the ages of eighteen and forty-nine, drank 500 million cases of the yellow stuff. That made Mountain Dew the sixth best-selling soft drink in the industry. Mountain Dew's fast-paced, in-your-face commercials have been so successful that two years later, the "Dew" climbed even higher—to the number four slot.

The reason may have more to do with the *subtext* of the commercials than with the citrus taste, however. After all, Mountain Dew had been around for years. But the "Do the Dew" commercials are relatively recent, having begun in the 1990s. Skydivers, snowboarders, bungee jumpers, and skateboarders performing extreme stunts symbolize a certain kind of lifestyle. And that is what Pepsico Inc., the makers of Mountain Dew, are really selling. That daring, life-on-the-

All advertisements have a subtext, or an underlying message. It is never stated directly. Instead, the subtext is implied or suggested through the use of symbols—characters, words, images, music, special effects—used to construct the message.

edge James Bond association is no coincidence. It is the subtext. *If you want to live the extreme life,* the subtext suggests, *then you gotta "Do the Dew."*

The challenge for any advertising copywriter or producer, then, is to figure out the right combination of symbols and subtext to create an overwhelming "want" in the consumer. Lifestyle advertisements are just one way to create a "want" in the consumer. Here are three other "want-to-have" techniques:

The Slice of Life Technique. A hapless office clerk receives an ultimatum from his boss: by morning, come up with a plan to cut office costs. The bewildered clerk can think of nothing. He doodles in his notebook, does push-ups on his office floor while the cleaning staff vacuums around him, even beats his head against the wall. Finally, he falls asleep with his head on a catalogue from Staples office supplies. In the morning when his boss knocks on the door, the clerk sleepily lifts his head—with the catalogue stuck to it. "Staples?" says the boss. "Why, you're a genius!"

Slice-of-life ads like the one just described tell a story, complete with characters, setting, and even a conflict. Of course, the bewildered clerk is no genius. That's the humor of the ad. The subtext of the ad, however, is serious: *If you want to save money, buy from Staples.*

The Demonstration Technique. On a sunny day at the beach, kids laugh and squeal with excitement as they toss and catch

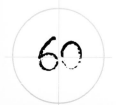

…and it'll get you dates, too. Mountain Dew doesn't claim to give you superhuman skateboarding skills *or* success in attracting a mate, but it *does* advertise a lifestyle.

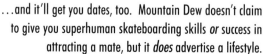

do the dew.

Flipballs. Of course, some have to dive face first into the sand to catch the ball on the peg, but that's part of the fun. Meanwhile, on other television channels children are hopping effortlessly down the sidewalk on Pogoballs, boys are zooming Turbo Tricksters across kitchen floors, and little girls are playing make-believe with a miniature Barbie Ice Cream Shoppe.

Demonstration advertisements show how a product works. With toys, the "want" comes in showing other children having fun playing with the products. *If you want to have fun like us*, the ad claims, *buy our toys*. With other products, like the Bounty paper towel once known as the "quicker picker upper," the want comes from seeing how well the product works. Often, commercial directors achieve some of that fun and effectiveness through editing. When *Consumer Reports* asked real kids to toss and catch Flipballs and hop down the street on Pogoballs, they couldn't do it…at least not easily. Either the actors hired for the commercial practiced a whole lot to get it right or, more likely, an editor cut out of the film the goofs and blunders to show all of the fun and none of the frustration.

The Testimonial Technique. Paula Abdul sings and dances…while wearing Reebok sneakers. Michael Jordan shyly admits to two adoring women who are wondering *Briefs? Or Boxers?* that he wears Hanes underwear. Actor Candice Bergen thinks everybody who calls long distance ought to save dimes a minute by using MCI's telephone service.

What these advertisements share in common is an authority who recommends the product. The authority may be a doctor, a parent, or a celebrity like Paula Abdul or Michael Jordan. Wanting to sing and dance like Paula sells sneakers, even though the shoes don't come with a guarantee of musical talent. Neither briefs nor boxers or a particular brand of underwear can change a man's physical characteristics. Even so, wanting to be "like Mike" still sells underwear.

Each of these four ways to want—lifestyle, slice of life, demonstration, testimonial— have been developed into video commercials that play on television, into audio commercials that air on radio stations, or into print ads for newspapers and magazines. But there is still another way to want and it uses a different medium altogether.

The Interactive Experience. Welcome to Niketown. Part store, part museum, Niketown is a five-story building on Chicago's Michigan Avenue. On one floor is an open space designed as a high school gymnasium. On another floor is a video theater that runs Nike commercials continuously as if they were feature films. As shoppers and browsers wander through "town," they can stop to study displays of historic moments in Nike merchandising and technological history—like developing the first pair of Air Jordans for the former Chicago Bulls superstar.

There are Niketowns in a number of large cities in America— New York, San Francisco, Los Angeles, Seattle. While each store differs somewhat in size, the concept of creating the "want" remains the same. What appears to be entertainment or even history is really a giant, interactive advertisement. Only, instead of viewing it on television or seeing it in a magazine, the "wanter" gets to walk into the ad and become a player in it.

Nike isn't the only big business that uses interactive experience as an advertising technique. In Atlanta, home of Coca-Cola, thousands of tourists each week walk through the Coca-Cola "museum." They start on the third floor with the soft drink's invention in the late nineteenth century under the genius of Asa Chandler, who first marketed the syrupy drink as a health tonic. Here the company's early advertising efforts are framed and showcased, often behind glass, as if in an art gallery. Overhead is a huge conveyor belt of green glass Coke bottles. As the bottles inch across the room just out of reach, the tourists below move also down to the second floor, passing along the way antique

You are getting thirsty.... At the Coca-Cola museum in Atlanta,
Coke isn't just the real thing, it's the only thing.

vending machines and a 1950s nostalgic soda fountain that plays 1950s
rock and roll. They enter a dark room where a futuristic and interactive
display uses a laser beam to send fresh-brewed, cold Coke in an arc
from the machine into your waiting cup twenty feet away. Everywhere
are ads—print ads, video ads, and radio jingles made popular in the
1960s, 1970s, and 1980s. The tour ends on the first floor in a gift shop
where tourists can buy glasses, mugs, serving trays, and clothing bear-
ing the Coca-Cola logo.

It's not Disney World, which remains the most colossal and im-
pressive of advertising acreage, but it's still an *experience*. It's fun, it's
even educational, and it makes you want to buy a Coke. And that, of
course, is the whole idea.

THE WEASELS

Advertising and the Law

It was a case for the advertising police.

In a 1990 television commercial, a monster truck roared over a line of cars parked one beside the other. Under the truck's powerful tires, car hoods folded and windshields shattered. One vehicle, however, remained remarkably intact. Manufactured by Volvo, the station wagon resisted the monster truck's crunching jaws. The demonstration seemed to prove Volvo's advertising claim that their cars are the safest on the road.

The folks at the Federal Trade Commission—known as the FTC—weren't convinced, however. Volvo cars may well have been the safest on the road, but the demonstration itself seemed suspicious. The FTC investigated. Sure enough, what the television viewer did not see and could not possibly know was that prior to filming, the advertisers had reinforced the Volvo with metal braces so that it alone would not crumple like a recyclable aluminum can. That was deceptive advertising, the FTC concluded, and not fair to the competition. Volvo apologized for misleading the public. The commercial did not run again.

Founded in 1914 by an act of Congress, the Federal Trade Commission really is the advertising police. The men and women who serve on the FTC review advertisements that appear on television and in print. They also read and review product labels, ensuring that advertising claims and nutritional information is not deceptive. Sometimes a consumer or a business will contact the FTC with a complaint. Other times a newspaper article or televised news story triggers an investigation. If the FTC believes a violation of the law has occurred, then it may take the advertiser and the company it represents to court or it may simply ask the offender to stop the illegal practice. Either way, the FTC has protected the consumer from advertising lies.

So, according to media literacy author Ivan Preston, that must mean you aren't fully clean unless you are zestfully clean. Right?

Not exactly.…

Advertisers often get around the law and the FTC by using **weasels**. A weasel is a word or a phrase presented in a sneaky way to sell a product or service. The weasel helps to make an advertising claim sound like a proven fact. American Airlines used a weasel in this advertising slogan: "Something special in the air." The weasel is the word *special*. What sounds like a fact is really puffery, an inflated claim about the airline. Something is in the air, all right—jets! But whether American's jets are special is someone's opinion.

According to FTC rules, advertisers can include weasels to puff up a product. The puffery may be false (something special really isn't in the air), but as long as the claim isn't deceptive, the advertiser hasn't broken the law.

Hold it. How can an advertisement be false but not deceptive? Aren't false and deceptive the same thing? Not in the land of advertisements!

Take product names, for example. The FTC assumes most people know that Swiss cheese isn't necessarily made in Switzerland or that Danish pastry isn't baked in Denmark, says author Preston. The FTC also assumes that most people realize meat shrinks when it is cooked. Therefore, when served, McDonald's Quarter Pounder, which weighs less than the four ounces the name suggests, is just a false name and not deceptive advertising.

Products that claim to offer the user some social or psychological benefit may also be false but not deceptive. The makers of Frosted Mini-Wheats claim their cereal is "For the adult in you, for the kid in you." But none of the ingredients listed on the cereal box, not even the added chemicals, actually triggers a childhood memory or kidlike re-action. The advertisers are making a social or emotional claim, not stating a fact.

Then there are the **mock-ups**. A mock-up is also a type of ad-vertising weasel. The image-maker alters the product in some way in order to film it or photograph it. For example, everyone knows that ice cream melts quickly, especially under the hot lights used during a pho-tographic shoot or the filming of a television commercial. Food make-up artists create yummy-looking dishes of ice cream using scoops of lard or mashed potatoes instead. To achieve a frothy-looking foam on a glass of beer, they might use shampoo suds. To redden a piece of steak that has been turning gray under hot lights all morning, they might paint the meat with Mercurochrome, a red-colored medicine ordinarily used for cuts and scrapes. Even though the advertisers do not tell the

On a hot day, there's nothing like a good, old-fashioned scoop of…lard?   Please pass the Mercurochrome…er, meat.

Super Weasels

Unless Mother Nature has been keeping secrets from scientists, iguanas do not talk, drink beer, or plot to assassinate swamp frogs in order to become television stars. Yet that is exactly what Louie the Lizard did in a commercial that aired during Super Bowl XXXII in January 1998.

Sometimes a weasel is an obviously impossible situation. But at an airtime cost of $1.3 million per thirty-second spot (or $43,400.00 per second) it's a super weasel!

Not every company has the multimillion dollar advertising budget to make it into advertising's big league—Super Bowl Sunday. Each year, the game draws a national television audience of more than 100 million viewers. An audience that large doesn't come cheap. On average, advertisers pay more than $1 million for each thirty-second spot and companies like Budweiser will buy as many as four spots during the game. Advertisers with that kind

viewer that they have drizzled chocolate syrup over iced mashed potatoes, which is clearly false advertising, it is not deceptive. According to the FTC, substituted products and alterations like these are all legal, but only because the advertiser could not photograph or film their products under ordinary circumstances. After swimming in milk for thirty minutes, most cereal flakes become soggy. If the image-maker uses glue instead of milk, the flakes stay crispy all day long, and the advertising police look the other way.

They didn't look away, however, when the 1990 Volvo commercial aired. That, too, was a mock-up. The image-maker altered the body of the car prior to filming in order to achieve a special effect. Why, *of money take their super weasels very seriously. At stake is more than a product, it's the company's reputation. In fact, that's just what McDonald's has called its Super Bowl ads—"reputation" spots, says* USA Today *reporter Martha T. Moore. The more humorous or more clever the ad, the more impressed the fans are.*

Louie the Lizard's Super Bowl assassination foul-up not only earned him top honors in the USA Today *Ad Meter for 1998 but also his own web page and screen saver. But fame can be short-lived. Who remembers the Budweiser Clydesdale horses playing their own football game and kicking for a field goal? It came in fourth place during Super Bowl XXX in 1996. Or the McDonald's dinosaur that did tricks for french fries, another Super Bowl XXX favorite? Or the boy on the beach who sucked himself through a straw right into a Pepsi bottle?*

They're advertising history now.

then, did the FTC find Volvo guilty of deceiving its viewers? Is that alteration any different than dabbing red medicine on a T-bone? Well, yes, said the FTC. First, the weasel wasn't an obvious falsity like Michael Jordan banking a basketball off the Goodyear blimp. Second, by showing its competitors' cars crumpling without revealing why the Volvo remained sound was misleading.

So what does all this mean? Weasels create puffery. Puffery is false but it is not always deceptive. Maybe nothing really does beat a great pair of L'eggs. The best thing about waking up just might be Folger's coffee in your cup. And maybe dogs do love Nissan trucks.

Then again, maybe not.

Part 4

JOLTS PER MINUTE

Media's Scare 'n Suspense Tactics

"The idea of having somebody on stage telling their side of the story and having the other person behind the stage…so that you can see the reaction as the other person is like, dissing them,…does so much for the energy of the show." So says television talk-show host Ricki Lake.[8]

By humiliating or belittling a person or by pitting two people against one another—whether both are on stage or one is backstage—Ricki Lake can whip her audience into a shouting frenzy. The confrontations always center on relationships—a cheating boyfriend, an out-of-control teenager, a mother who abandoned her children. Often the "energy" explodes into fist fights or guests throwing chairs at one another. The electrified audience cheers for the ambushed underdog.

This is real life folks, Jerry Springer tells his audience, don't you love it? They answer by chanting "JER-RY, JER-RY." They have loved it so much that in 1998, the Jerry Springer Show soared to the number one spot for afternoon programming. Off camera, Springer admits his show is "silly" and "outrageous."

Television talk shows aren't the only venues where media wizards use confrontations or fear, violence, and vengeance to shock the American public into watching a program or buying a newspaper or magazine. From emotional ambushes on an afternoon talk show to news stories of children who kill, from undercover investigations into unseen dangers in commonly used products like painkillers, to the grisly

"JER-RY, JER-RY". . . Jerry Springer's show often features foul-mouthed, violent guests who don't seem to have much to say that's intelligent, and who are set up so messy confrontations are almost inevitable. Wouldn't it be a relief to find out that the media wizards had taken it one step further and made up the stories and hired actors to play the guests?

special effects of TV's *ER,* to the over-the-top antics of professional wrestlers, media wizards are experts at pushing our emotional buttons. They even have a code word for it: **jolts per minute.**

Some wizards justify their JPMs by saying their programs are simply a reflection of our increasing violent times. Don't you believe it, says the Center for Media and Public Affairs. According to a study they conducted, murder was the number one topic on network evening news programs between 1992 and 1996 despite statistics that showed crime in America had actually decreased during that same period.

Ricki Lake's observation provides a clue to the real reason behind the media jolts: money. JPMs create energy; without energy there would be no viewers; without viewers (also called ratings), there would be no advertisers; without advertisers, there would be no profits.

FRAMING VIOLENCE IN JONESBORO

Episodic Versus Thematic News Frames

On March 24, 1998, at 12:35 in the afternoon, the fire alarm in Westside Middle School in the small town of Jonesboro, Arkansas, suddenly rang. Some students grinned in anticipation of a few free minutes away from their desks; others groaned at having to practice still another fire drill. Moments later, however, as teachers and students filed from the building into the school playground, gunfire exploded from a nearby wood.

At first, some students thought the noise was firecrackers. But then one, two, three students fell as the rapid fire continued. This was no practice drill. It was a deliberately planned ambush by two boys who had skipped school that morning. Dressed in camouflage clothing and crouched under cover of sage grass and oak saplings, Mitchell Johnson, thirteen, and Andrew Golden, eleven, took aim at their classmates who were trapped inside the playground's chain-linked fence. They fired twenty-two rounds of ammunition in less than four minutes, and then fled.

Ambushed by the media in their haste to cover the story, a Westside Middle School student tells what she witnessed during the Jonesboro, Arkansas, shootings.

The Jonesboro shooting was a terrible tragedy. It was also what journalists call *breaking news*, an event that becomes known even as the story is still unfolding. Breaking news travels fast. Within minutes following the frantic 911 calls from Westside Middle School, local news reporters in Jonesboro and surrounding areas became aware of the emergency situation and the police response. A national news agency called the Associated Press (AP) also picked up the story and transmitted it over its wire service to thousands of news outlets across the country. One of those outlets was the CNN television studios in Atlanta, Georgia, more than five hundred miles from Jonesboro. In a news bulletin, anchor Lou Waters announced the shooting. According to the AP wire he had just received, as many as thirteen children had been injured, Waters reported.

Less than twenty minutes had passed from the time Andrew Golden had pulled the fire alarm to when CNN's news bulletin reported the awful ambush.

Behind the scenes at CNN, segment producers were already on the telephone and the Internet, trying to piece together the details of the story. Segment producers do not write the news or report it, but they are journalists just the same. Called "bookers," they locate people who have been affected in some way by a news event and who will agree to an on-air interview. The nonfiction world of journalism is a competitive place with dozens of magazines stacked on newsstand shelves and hundreds of cable television channels available by the push of a remote control button. Being "scooped" means losing the story, and therefore the audience, to a competitor. Journalism's credo is to inform, yes. But the need to "hook and hold" an audience is equally essential. To inform an audience, you must first get their attention.

That's where the news *frame* can help.

There is a difference between a newsworthy event and news coverage of an event. News—even breaking news—doesn't just happen. It is *mediated*. The story broadcast over television is not a mirror image of what happened but rather a constructed interpretation of the incident. Coverage of even a tragic incident like the Jonesboro shootings will vary significantly, depending on the selected news frame.

Episodic reporting focuses on people and events, piecing together journalism's jigsaw puzzle: *Who did what to whom and why.* The public learns of a news event through televised news bulletins and special reports or through page one headlines and news stories of multiple paragraphs. The coverage is usually brief and to the point and the images accompanying the story are action driven and dramatic: scenes of fires, earthquake damage, flooding rivers, and yes, trembling children in shock after surviving a shooting ambush.

Thematic reporting, on the other hand, focuses on ideas, exploring broader social issues and patterns behind a news event. The coverage is more in-depth and requires more airtime or print space, and therefore is presented most often as television documentaries or in magazine feature stories or books. The images are less action driven. Instead, the stories often feature experts—doctors, teachers, lawyers—who share and debate points of view. Media wizards often refer to this less-exciting visual presentation as "talking heads."

Because television is such a visual medium, episodic reporting is an excellent way to jolt an audience into attention. CNN was not alone in its frenzied attempts to get episodic news and images for its updates through the afternoon of March 24 and in the days following the shooting. Reporters and photographers from every major television network and newspaper group descended upon Jonesboro, intent on revealing who did what to whom and why.

In bits and pieces through news bulletins and news briefs, the public learned the shocking details. Four girls and a teacher had been killed in the gunplay. Dozens of other children, all girls except for one, had been wounded. One of the shooters, Mitchell Johnson, had been rejected by a girl who did not want him as a boyfriend. He had sworn revenge. Some children had heard that Mitchell was going to shoot somebody. Nobody believed he would really do it except perhaps for the twelve-year-old girl who had rejected Mitchell. She had escaped injury.

It was also breaking news.

A **frame** is how an image-maker presents or arranges the elements in a fiction or nonfiction story. Journalists can approach a story by framing it either as **episodic** reporting or **thematic** reporting. The difference between the two framing techniques is important because the frame determines how much and what kind of information the public receives.

Days after the incident, the flood of stories continued. As long as there were emotionally charged eyewitness accounts to retell and images to show—the funerals for the dead girls and their teacher, the surviving students of Westside returning to class—Jonesboro remained an episodic news story.

So much coverage might give the impression that the media was doing a thorough investigative report. In fact, they were filling airtime and print space with variations of the same episodic reports. Missing from many of the episodic stories or buried within them were statistics that revealed juvenile crime involving guns had actually been in decline since 1994; that school shootings had also dropped significantly since 1992. Those more reassuring studies were lost in the echo of the episodic headlines of the incident: AMERICANS BEWILDERED BY THEIR BABY-FACED KILLERS (*London Times*, March 26, 1998), HOSPITAL MET CARNAGE OF KIDS (*Arkansas Democrat-Gazette*, March 25, 1998); ARKANSAS BURIES ITS DEAD (*ABC TV news*, March 29, 1998); WHAT IS JUSTICE FOR A SIXTH GRADE KILLER? (*Time*, March 31, 1998).

The sheer number of articles about Jonesboro and other school killings over a two-year period had a stunning effect. The public was

The CNN newsroom—where news is mediated.

frightened. Were America's schools safe? Were today's adolescents a deeply troubled generation? Most importantly, people began to ask, why do children kill?

Those questions could not be answered in short, episodic stories. Those questions required thematic reporting, stories that explore the causes and effects of violence. Thematic stories take time to research. Unlike episodic stories that travel fast, thematic stories often don't surface until weeks or months have passed. By then, however, the event has faded from the TV screens. The need to hook and hold an audience remains, but the story isn't current or "breaking news" any longer. Some other jolting story may have taken its place.

Six months after the shooting, an Arkansas judge sentenced Andrew Golden and Mitchell Johnson for the murders they committed. On that day, August 12, 1998, radio news commentator Ray Suarez hosted a forty-eight-minute talk show over National Public Radio focusing on violent children. His story had a thematic frame. The "booked" interviewees were not traumatized teachers and students but rather Charles Aaron, a criminal defense attorney from Chicago who specializes in juvenile crime, and James Garbarino, codirector of the Family Development Center at Cornell University. Discussion during the program focused not on Andrew Golden and Mitchell Johnson specifically, but rather on the social environments that foster violence in children like Andrew and Mitchell.

Charles Aaron made this important and thoughtful distinction about violent children: "There is a difference between a juvenile who commits a crime and a criminal who commits a crime as a juvenile." Aaron's statement was idea oriented, not event oriented.

The second guest, James Garbarino, shared this insight with the audience: "Each week I sit with kids who are in prison or on trial for murder and I am struck by how often, how very often, you can see a mental health problem in their childhood that was not cared for. By the time the child is eight years old, he has gotten wrapped up in a pattern of very negative, anti-social behavior."

Garbarino's comment is also idea oriented. Children who in early childhood were or felt they were rejected, said Gabarino, don't operate under the same emotional controls as other children. Most children who kill come from this group. "And that," stressed Garbarino, "puts a different slant on the story of kids who just suddenly show up and are bad." Garbarino also pointed out that 90 percent of the children who kill are boys. Why? Attempting to answer *that* question, he said, can help us get to the root of the problem. Getting to the root of the problem is what thematic reporting is all about.[9]

The way media wizards frame the news is important because it determines how much and what kind of information the public receives. Recognizing the difference between episodic and thematic reporting is also important because the frame affects the public's perception of violence. Television and newspapers, due to time and space limits and the need to hook and hold their audiences, report crime and violence most frequently through episodic frames. The result, however, can be a misleading belief that crime is on the rise and children are becoming more and more violent. Millions of American viewers tuned in to watch CNN's news updates in the hours and days following the Jonesboro shootings. Millions more saw other televised coverage and read the hundreds of print and magazine articles. But how many of those same viewers also heard Attorney Aaron and Dr. Garbarino's discussions that explosions of violence in children like Mitchell Johnson and Andrew Golden are neither common nor sudden nor without some disturbing childhood cause?

Episodic news frames aren't all bad. But without thematic frames to further the understanding of the issues behind the news events, balance in the news is like a playground teeter-totter with no one sitting on the opposite seat.

SCARE TACTICS

How Infotainment Packages News as Stories

Open your mouth. Say "Ahhh!" See any silver fillings in there? If you do, you may be the victim of mercury amalgam poisoning.

At least, that was the suggestion of the December 23, 1990, *60 Minutes* story broadcast by CBS television news anchor Morley Safer. Was Safer intentionally frightening his audience with news that the mercury amalgam, or mixture, used in silver dental fillings could be slowly releasing toxins into the human body? Certainly the segment title "Poison in Your Mouth" was scary. And the real people interviewed during the segment had compelling, if not frightening, stories to tell. One woman who had suffered for years from multiple sclerosis, a disease that attacks the body's nervous system, claimed that her symptoms disappeared "overnight" once her dentist removed the silver fillings from her mouth.

The familiar ticking stopwatch of the granddaddy of all newsmagazines, *60 Minutes*

It could never have happened, said Stephen Barrett, M.D. Mercury poisoning doesn't just disappear from the human body overnight. It may seem like a small detail, but it was huge to Dr. Barrett. He thought the *60 Minutes* segment was "the most irresponsible report on a health topic ever broadcast on network television." And he wrote a letter to the show's producer, Don Hewitt, to tell him so. Didn't Morley Safer know that studies since the early 1900s had shown that "fewer than fifty cases of allergy to the amalgam have been reported in the scientific literature"? Apparently Morley Safer did know. But he also had the words of a number of dentists who believed that a link did exist between mercury poisoning and disease, including arthritis, in some patients.

Barrett accused *60 Minutes* of using scare tactics.

Hewitt wrote back that the show had been fair and balanced, presenting arguments on both sides of the issue.

Case closed, right? Well, not exactly.

Later studies, one conducted by the U. S. Department of Health and Human Services in 1993 and another by the American Dental Association in 1998, revealed no health consequences from mercury amalgam. However, *60 Minutes* did not broadcast another feature story segment to share these new findings with their viewers. Maybe it wasn't newsy enough. Or maybe...it wasn't scary enough.

When *60 Minutes* first flashed across the television screens of America in the late 1960s, the program, with its ticking stopwatch, was unlike any other news show of the time. Its format was broadcast journalism, and for at least twenty years, it ruled the roost of serious, in-depth news reporting. Times and television have changed, however. Now *60 Minutes* has big competition from a whole lineup of newsmagazines, as they're known, including *20/20, Hard Copy, 48 Hours, Inside Edition,* and *Prime Time Live.*

Newsmagazine-type programs are cheaper to produce than most hour-long dramas, costing a mere $700,000 per single episode while still earning impressive profits for the networks. An hour-long drama, on the other hand, can rack up more than a million dollars if the show is a big hit like *ER*. That's a key reason why all major networks began airing more and more editions of their newsmagazines in the 1990s.

Newsmagazines follow a formula that has generated a new media code word: **infotainment**. The stars of the show are news commentators who present feature news—rather than breaking news—in an entertaining way, most often by telling a story. Like all stories, conflict and characters are the very heart of the telling. The program usually opens with a scare-tactic teaser. It may be a question: "What do you need to know about avoiding highway pileup?" (*20/20*, 1998). It may be the segment's title that triggers alarm, like: "Poisons in the Playground" about chemicals in pressure-treated wood (*Hard Copy*, 1997) or "A Deadly Mix" about mixing Tylenol and alcohol (*Prime Time Live*, 1995). Or it may be the commentator's *lead-in*, or introduction, that raises apprehension, such as this:

In a country of 17,000 islands, a ferry chugging safely along is more than just a welcome sight. It's a lifeline. Indonesians depend on them. Here no one worries when heavy cargo is loaded on board or when a ferry is overcrowded. No one believes that anything will go seriously wrong. But something did—last January in a place called Banda Aceh. (Dateline, September 16, 1998).

Scare tactics are marketing hype to hook viewers into watching. The scare may prove to be not as dreadful as first suggested. And the scare is not always about bodily damage or threat of death as in the Tylenol and alcohol stories. It might be a consumer red alert, such as an investigation into new car dealers who overcharge their customers.

Feature news stories differ from breaking news in this way: Features are not as timely as breaking news; the goal of feature stories is to entertain as well as to inform. Often features allow an image-maker to provide more in-depth coverage of an interesting event or news personality.

Once the story begins, the on-screen video takes the viewer to the setting of the story and introduces the characters whose conflicts are the focus of the report. At various points, the narrative pauses while a witness or a source provides comments on the person or the situation. A *20/20* report from September 1998 by John Quinones on one woman's struggle with sexual harassment in the workplace began with a description of the victim, Teri Lohr:

> *John Quinones—Teri, who so loved her nieces and neph-*
> *ews, seemed to have the world at her feet—[she was] beau-*
> *tiful, exuberant, responsible.*
> *Maggie McColins— She wanted it all. And she had it all.*
> *She liked the nice things in life—furniture, cars...*

Although the stories are true, the way the facts are presented—as a story being retold or reenacted—is what makes the program infotainment and not strictly news. If *60 Minutes* were to broadcast "Poison in Your Mouth" today using this narrative framework, the content of the program would shift. Morley Safer might still include two sides of the argument, but the focus would be on the character and her conflict. The lead, or opening in which the hook is planted, might go something like this:

> *Multiple sclerosis . . . It attacks the brain and the nervous system, debilitating its victims with days and nights of tortured pain. The cause of the disease is still not proved, but some dentists have a theory—mercury amalgam poisoning. It is a theory the American Dental Association has rejected. Tonight, one woman's courageous struggle back to health and the doctor who risked his medical career to help her.*

OK, so it *is* a little melodramatic, but the formula works. If it didn't, people wouldn't watch and the millions of dollars in advertising profits would swiftly slip away. So, what's the problem? Surely, entertainment—even infotainment—has a place on television.

One problem might be this: In a Gallup Poll from the late 1990s, most Americans named TV newsmagazines as the medium they trusted the most to deliver the truth about the news. They rated newsmagazines higher than nightly newscasts and local newspapers. But in order to make the news entertaining, the media wizards heighten the drama and the suspense. In other words, they alter the reality of the story to make it more suspenseful or more amusing or more terrifying than it might actually be.

Even the producer of *60 Minutes*, Don Hewitt, has some trouble with that approach. "I wish we were still in the business of reporting news," he said. "I'm afraid a lot of us are now in the business of filling time." Of course, loyal Hewitt maintains that *60 Minutes*, the oldest newsmagazine of the bunch, is still the best at reporting news as news and not as entertainment.

There may be another problem. Like minute bits of mercury in a silver tooth filling, entertainment is slowly leaking into all aspects of television news. The election of national leaders, the education of children, even religion are at risk of becoming infotainment. Has the American public become so used to being entertained that they simply aren't interested in anything that *isn't* entertainment? Is the only way to get their attention on any subject by jolting them with scare tactics and consumer red alerts?

Now *that* could be

a really

scary story.

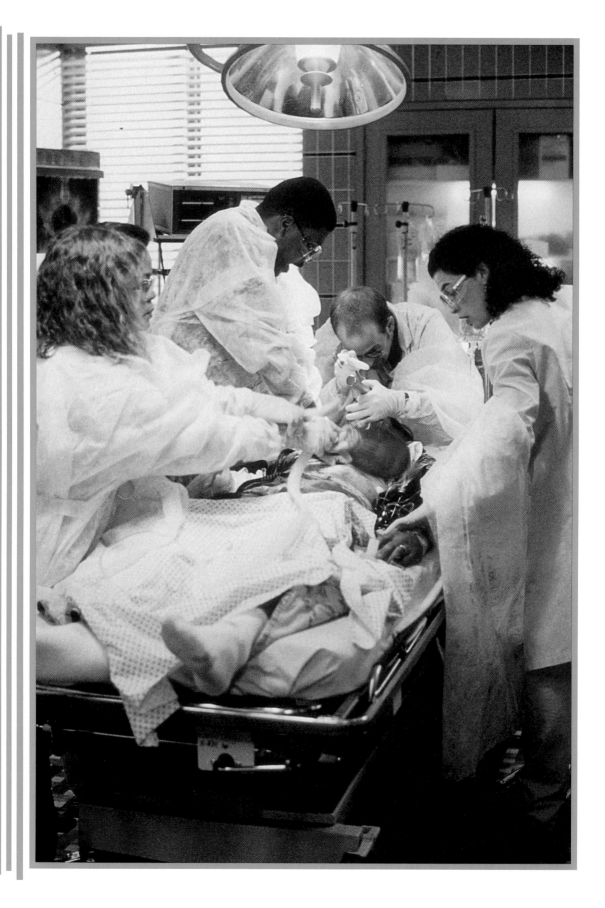

BLOOD 'N GUTS 'N LIQUID PLASTIC

Creating Reality on TV's ER

One day while actor Anthony Edwards was flying from New York to Los Angeles a flight attendant said to him, "Too bad you weren't on yesterday's flight. A woman suffered a stroke." Edwards responded with disbelief. "Why would you wish *me* at 30,000 feet when a woman is having a stroke?"

Anthony Edwards is not a doctor, but he plays one on TV.

As Dr. Mark Greene on NBC's dramatic series *ER*, Edwards has sutured wounds, suctioned throats, and paddle-shocked unbreathing patients back to life again. Naturally, performing emergency procedures on a stroke victim in flight across the country would be in keeping with his character. With his character, yes; with the actor, no way.

The fast-paced action on *ER* looks and sounds so real that people often mistake the characters, including those bloodied bodies writhing on hospital gurneys, for the real thing. Although the medical instruments are real, the lacerations, bruises, and heart attacks are pure Hollywood special effects. For example, liquid plastic poured into molds

The drama and special effects on *ER* are so real, they're scary. But don't confuse actor Anthony Edwards (second from right) with a real doctor.

makes a batch of phony wounds and scars of various sizes that a makeup artist can glue onto an actor's body. The actor-doctor stitches away through the supple plastic without ever piercing real-life muscle or skin.

Should the script call for an arm amputation, there's no problem. The special effects team creates prosthetics, or human body parts, also made of plastic. In this particular scene, an actress played the role of a traffic accident victim. The makeup artist "strapped" a prosthetic shoulder onto the actress, then secured a false arm to the stump end of the shoulder. Next came the body makeup. Dabs and streaks of blues and grays, reds and purples suggested that the woman's arm was nearly severed from the shoulder. To complete the grisly makeup, the artist mixed corn syrup, which is just the right thickness to simulate human blood, with food coloring. During the amputation scene, the actor-doctor cut away the fake arm from the fake shoulder while the fake patient provided very real cries and moans.

So realistic are the special effects that one of the staff who works on the show has said, "I have to keep telling myself this is make-believe."

ER is media wizardry of a different kind. The show's JPMs, however, involve a lot more than just corn-syrup blood and liquid plastic lacerations. Whereas newsmagazines package their real-life features as stories with characters and settings and conflicts, *ER* presents its stories as if they were real life. To create the show's reality-based situations, the team of writers interview practicing doctors and nurses in emergency rooms across the country and delve into medical journals. Professional doctors are among the show's technical advisers. They provide insight to how a doctor might treat a patient suffering from traumatic injuries and teach the actors how to properly handle the medical instruments, how to pronounce really long medical terms like idopathic thombocytopenia purpura, and how to speak emergency room lingo. "Call for O Neg, 15 units, stat!" means the shooting victims just wheeled in need blood transfusions—now!

Creating realism through special effects, real emergency situations, and dialogue that also rings true keeps more than 60 million viewers around the world tuning into the one-hour drama week after week. That's just the way the show's producer, Michael Crichton, had envisioned the show when it was still an idea in his head. Crichton, who graduated from Harvard Medical School, had worked in a hospital emergency room where each day was "continuous havoc." He wanted to recapture that fast-paced, high-pressure environment on a dramatic television series.

Crichton's concept for the drama, however, frightened the network executives at NBC, those who decide which pilots actually become series. Other medical shows had been successful, but they focused more on the doctors' personal lives once they had removed their white coats and stethoscopes. Crichton's show focused on the patients—as many as a dozen medical cases introduced each week—and the difficult decisions the medical staff had to make to treat those patients. Would such a show be able to earn a large *market share*, or percentage of the viewing audience across the country, to place it high in the overall television ratings?

The two-hour pilot that introduced Chicago's fictional County General Hospital and its medical staff had more than eighty-seven scenes and more than one hundred speaking parts. During rehearsals, Crichton pushed the actors to "rattle off" their lines, shouting, "Faster! Faster!"

The network executives who viewed the two-hour pilot were confused. The show didn't have a primary plotline focusing on just one character; instead it had many, a new one for each new medical emergency that arose. Nor was there a traditional beginning, middle, and end to each story. When the viewer first entered the emergency room, the action was already in progress. What followed was a series of small scenes, or montages. One montage focused on the victims of a building that had collapsed. Another revealed a doctor comforting a cancer patient. Through the camera's eye, the viewer wandered from one ex-

myself this is
make-believe."

amination room to another, peering behind each curtain. As a team of doctors, nurses, and technicians worked feverishly on a patient, the television camera filming the action circled the gurney, giving the impression that the viewer was actually in the room, circling, too, to get a better look at what was happening. Even when the pilot ended, the action didn't. The final scene showed nurse Carol Hathaway being wheeled into the emergency room, the victim of a drug overdose. As much as the viewer wanted to see what happened next, Crichton abruptly drew the curtain.

"The show broke rules," Crichton admitted without any apologies. "The script I had was honest-to-God real life. . . ." That realism, says Crichton, "terrified" some network people.[10]

Even Noah Wyle, the actor who plays Dr. John Carter, had his doubts. "I was thinking this is a great show but seven episodes in, they're going to cancel us."

"No one had a tremendous amount of confidence in the pilot at the time that we did it," Michael Crichton agreed.

But that was then—before a *Newsweek* cover story, before the Emmy awards, and before Anthony Edwards had ever stitched a plastic leg wound or could rattle off "idopathic thombocytopenia purpura" without stumbling over the words.

Now flight attendants are reassured whenever he boards a plane.

RAGE IN A CAGE

How Sports, Stereotypes, and Soap Opera Butt Heads in the Big Ring

When Joanie was a little girl growing up in Rochester, New York, her brothers used to wrestle inside the dog kennel in the backyard. In these cage matches, the boys imitated the television stars of the World Wrestling Federation (WWF). Joanie loved sports, all kinds of sports. But wrestling was different. "I thought it was the stupidest thing and that it was for guys," she said. Even so, she joined the game by making championship belts out of tinfoil for whomever won the match inside the dog cage.

That was one of Joanie's lives. Graduating with honors from high school and studying Spanish literature at the University of Tampa, Florida, was her other life. Joanie's dream was to work for the Peace Corps or join the Secret Service as an agent. You might say her dream came true. Joanie has gone undercover as "Chyna," only it's not the United States government she is protecting. It's the WWF's DeGeneration-X, a team of professional wrestlers.

When Chyna strides calmly into an arena—wearing a sleeveless black leather vest, black boots, and black shades—the fans take notice.

So do the wrestlers in the ring. Chyna commands respect, in part because her body is so incredibly powerful but also in part because she is so coolly self-controlled. She doesn't smile. She rarely speaks. There are those fans who jeer her but she never cracks. She's there to do a job: protect DX superstars Shawn "The Heartbreak Kid" Michaels, the Road Dog, and X-Pac. No one wrestles dirty and gets away with it when Chyna is in the house.

"Chyna is the ultimate last resort when help is needed," she said. "DX can usually take care of themselves, but when needed, she's there."

It's all an act, of course. It's a game, just like wrestling in the dog cage with her brothers, only now it's in front of millions of fans and television viewers and for a whole lot more than just a tinfoil belt. Now it isn't stupid. Now it's thrilling.

Chyna doesn't wrestle other women. That's not her style. She is a bouncer, the backbone of the DX team. "The first time I stepped into the ring with Shawn . . . and heard the big cheer from the crowd…I thought, 'Oh, my God, is that really me?' or 'Am I really part of this?' It doesn't seem real sometimes."

Just what is real and what is fake about world wrestling?

For one thing, the money is real. Fans spend millions and not just on tickets for the explosive live events. The wrestling federation has licensed T-shirts and hats, gym bags and backpacks, videos and posters and magazines. Then there are also federation wristwatches, beach blankets, and cue sticks; life-size cardboard stand-ups of superstars, a 900 telephone hot line featuring a different star each day and…well, you get the idea. Spending doesn't stop at ringside.

The wrestling is real. Sure, it's entertainment. The wrestlers themselves admit it. "Three and a half hours of non-stop, completely out of this world entertainment," is how Mike "The Hitman" Hart puts it. But it is also a sport. Those scoop slams to the mat and double clotheslines over the ropes are choreographed and practiced as in any sport, but they are crunchingly right on. So are the dropkicks, body slams, stand-

He may be onto something here. Jesse "The Body" Ventura takes down Hulk Hogan in his former career as a professional wrestler. Elected governor of Minnesota in 1998, Ventura now "takes down" political opponents. Since pro wrestling is a delicate balance of hard-hitting action and plain old theatrics, perhaps a career in politics isn't much of a stretch for him. Can politicians-turned-pro wrestlers be far behind?

ing leg drops, big splashes, and avalanches. So are the injuries. Check out this lead paragraph from an article written by Kevin Kelly about D'Lo Brown's injuries during a match against Dan "The Beast" Severn: "His chest snapped like the wishbone at Thanksgiving. His pectoral muscles were ripped form the bone. He was in agony....His career was over..."

Or was it?

Many wrestlers enter the sport after a career-ending injury in pro football. Their weight and their athletic training translates well in the ring. Most study key moves with professional trainers. One of the best trainers in the business is a surly old man called Killer Kowalski. Killer's not his first name, but it might as well be. He's the one who sweated Chyna into shape and taught her the moves.

OK, so the money is real. The wrestling moves are real. What about the emotions? Dr. Death has boasted that he'll "deliver a heavy dose of pain and punishment" to anyone stupid enough to get in his way of winning the federation championship. The wrestler known as Crusher sits on the chest of his opponent, cutting off his breath. Another who calls himself Konnan grabs the microphone from the ringside officials and shouts at the fans. And the fans shout back. They cheer and jeer and laugh and applaud and hiss. In wrestling, attitude is a two-way street: from the ring to the seats and back again. Professional wrestling is "rage in a cage" and the fans love every minute.

The personas or personalities of the individual wrestlers, however, are not real. They're stereotyped images of villains, underdogs, and heroes. The matches are battles of good against evil, with grudge meetings a guarantee. "Basically, we are all human versions of super heroes," says Mike "The Hitman." He compares himself to Batman ("Only I'm a little better"). Hart believes in his character so much that he wears it home. "There are people who tend to make fun of me for taking [wrestling] so seriously, that I believe in my persona so much...but I do, and I always have," he says.

And then there's Chyna.

Within a year of joining the federation, Chyna had been dubbed "the fourth wonder of the world" and became a superstar in her own right. Like "The Hitman," Chyna may also be a comic-book stereotype—the Amazon, the woman warrior. Still, in portraying Chyna, Joanie has also broken a stereotype—the one that women don't belong in the sport of wrestling.

Joanie describes Chyna as if she is someone other than herself, and in a way, she is. "There's a mystery to Chyna. You never see her jumping up and down or really smiling. There is so much I can do with my character. She hasn't even been unleashed yet."

Chyna's persona—with Joanie's help—has changed the image of women in the sport. "Right now, what I do is very unique, and I'm at a level where I'm working with the guys on their level."

So what if she doesn't get to wear the big belt? She's main event.

Part Four

SMOKE AND MIRRORS

Urban Legends and Media Hoaxes

Oz the Great and Terrible understood one thing about the people who lived in the land of Oz— they were gullible. Why else would they lock on their green spectacles each time they entered the Emerald City? Emeralds did indeed stud the streets and side-walks, but their glare was not blinding. As Dorothy discovered, the glasses were a hoax.

A hoax is a trick, a fabrication about a person, place, or thing. Although false, something about the claim or the story rings true. Most successful hoaxes, or urban legends as modern folklorists call them, do in fact have a kernel of truth in them. But this kernel is embedded in exaggeration or outrageous circumstances that should—but don't always—signal a deception.

Very often a hoax or urban legend grows out of distrust or misunderstanding of others or of foreign places, alternative lifestyles, big business, or modern technology. Others are perpetrated on purpose for profit. Once begun, a hoax can spread like wildfire—either by word of mouth or also by the media, including the Internet.

The art of deceiving the public, however, isn't a late twentieth-century development. Before the Internet, before television, before radio, there lived perhaps the greatest real-life hoax master of all—P. T. Barnum.

L. Frank Baum might have based his character Oz the Great and Terrible on this real-life circus entertainer and promoter. Barnum, who earned and lost a fortune gambling on human gullibility, once said, "There's a sucker born every minute."

He used the media to prove it.

THE PRINCE OF HUMBUG

How P. T. Barnum Hoodwinked the World

A business acquaintance first told P. T. Barnum in the summer of 1835 about a woman named Joice Heth who had cared for young George Washington on his father's Virginia plantation. She had been a slave once owned by Augustus Washington, the father of the father of our country. If true—and a documented "original bill of sale" dating from February 5, 1727, seems to indicate that it was—then this remarkable woman was more than 160 years old!

The acquaintance showed Barnum an advertisement from *The Philadelphia Inquirer* that announced her appearance at Masonic Hall. It read: "The citizens of Philadelphia and its vicinity, have an opportunity of witnessing…one of the greatest natural curiosities ever witnessed, JOICE HETH…" Of course, the citizens of Philadelphia had to pay to "witness" (or see) Joice Heth. During the early nineteenth century, traveling exhibits, menageries, and circuses were a common form of entertainment.

Curious, Barnum traveled to Philadelphia to see the curiosity himself. The woman was so old and so frail she could not sit up. Barnum described her in his autobiography: "She was lying upon a high lounge in the middle of the room; her lower extremities were drawn up, with her knees elevated some two feet above the top of the lounge. She was apparently in good health and spirits, but…she was totally blind, and her eyes were so deeply sunken in their sockets that the eyeballs seemed to have disappeared altogether." Her fingernails, Barnum noted, were four inches long!

P. T. Barnum saw something more in Joice Heth than just an old woman. He saw opportunity. He purchased the exhibition rights and then began to "plant" stories about Heth in newspapers. She was pure of character, the news stories reported, and she had helped to mold the great qualities with which George Washington had led this country as president. Barnum recognized that it was Heth's relationship with Washington—not her age—that made her an attraction.

When she died a year later, an autopsy revealed the truth. She was simply an old woman, no more than eighty years of age. She had not even been born when George Washington was a child. Despite the deception or perhaps because of it, Joice Heth launched Barnum's career in the humbug business.

A **humbug** is a type of hoax. It is much more than just a lie. A master humbug will entertain as well as deceive the audience, and almost always pockets some coins for the effort. Before radio and television and motion pictures, humbugs were public amusements, and their advertisements were pure media manipulations. Because of the amazing collection of living curiosities he acquired and his equally amazing ability to use the media to his advantage, P. T. Barnum would soon become known throughout the world as the "Prince of Humbug."

A few years after Joice Heth's death, Barnum purchased a large building on the corner of Broadway and Ann Street in New York City. On New Year's Day, 1842, he officially opened Barnum's American

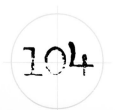

Museum. Museums at this time were not the homes of fine works of art or natural history artifacts. Most were "dime museums." For a ten-cent admission fee, a person could view an exotic animal from a far-away place, a living curiosity, or other unexplained oddities of nature. Barnum's American Museum, however, offered five floors of attractions, to which he charged a quarter admission. Among the landscape paintings and wax sculptures on display were albinos, giants, and a bearded lady. The visitors suddenly coming upon these living "freaks" were startled, but they could not look away. Barnum understood that a cruel bit of human nature is always drawn to the unusual, the exotic, the thing that is different from "us."

The "Feejee Maiden" was one. Caught by Japanese fishermen off the Fiji Islands in the South Pacific, the "maiden" was supposedly a mermaid. Barnum purchased it, then put his mind to work on how best to arouse public interest in the specimen. Once again, he planted stories, this time through anonymous letters sent to the editors of newspapers in Philadelphia and New York City. He wrote the letters himself, spreading rumors that such a creature existed. Then he mailed the letters to friends in southern cities with the instructions that they were to post the letters to editors there. "The corresponding post-marks did much to prevent suspicion of a hoax," he admitted.

Soon, the press was clamoring for a glimpse of the mermaid, in part to debunk it as a humbug. What they saw stunned them. Barnum describes the image in his autobiography:

> *The animal was an ugly, dried-up, black-looking, and diminutive specimen, about three feet long. Its mouth was open, its tail turned over, and its arms thrown up, giving it the appearance of having died in great agony. The spine of the fish proceeded in a straight and apparently unbroken line to the base of the skull—the hair of the animal was*

found growing several inches down on the shoulders of the fish, and the application of a microscope absolutely revealed what seemed to be minute fish scales lying in myriads amidst the hair.

The reporters could neither confirm that the specimen was a mermaid nor deny it. That was so much the better for Barnum. Now the public would have to come and judge for themselves. He printed 10,000 mermaid pamphlets and hired boys to sell them at a penny apiece in hotels and stores and on the streets.

"The mermaid fever was now getting pretty well up," Barnum said. That's when he placed his advertisement. "Positively for one week only!" the flyer further enticed the public. He worried a bit that some people might remember his Joice Heth hoax, but if they did, it mattered not. Crowds came and crowds paid. The humbug was a success. Years later, the truth came out. The FeeJee Maiden was really the head and body of a monkey grafted onto the tail of a large fish. Barnum admitted that, yes, the FeeJee Maiden had been "manufactured." But he was not the one who had concocted the creation. He had merely discovered it.

The American Museum was, in Barnum's own words, "the ladder by which I rose to fortune." Huge pictures of beasts and birds, creeping things, and other curiosities covered the outside of the building. The museum opened at sunrise and often tourists went there before eating breakfast. Some of his exhibits were not frauds. Chang and Eng were conjoined twins born in Siam (now Thailand). The term "Siamese twins" originated with them and Barnum's promotion. Madame Josephine Cloffulia was indeed a bearded lady. JoJo the Dog-Faced Boy was born in Russia with a rare condition in which hair grew over most of his face and body. Barnum, however, claimed that the sixteen-year-old had lived in forests and caves and ate small game. As part of the act, Barnum urged JoJo to bark and growl when in public.

Barnum's American Museum in New York City

One of Barnum's biggest assets was tiny Tom Thumb, shown here at his marriage to Lavinia Warren.

While these living curiosities were real, the stories Barnum concocted about them to drum up public interest were hoaxes. He continued to write fake letters. Often the letters accused P. T. Barnum of being a humbug and duping the public. The newspapers published the letters, not knowing they had been written by P. T. himself as publicity plants. So successful was Barnum at the art of humbug and so hungry were people to witness the world's oddities that within two years Barnum had paid for his museum, cleared all his debts, and had a surplus of money to boot.

The most successful humbug of all, and for Barnum the most interesting, was General Tom Thumb. His real name was Charles S. Stratton, and he was born in Bridgeport, Connecticut, in 1838. Barnum met him while passing through Bridgeport. There he heard stories of a "remarkably small child" in the city. Barnum sought him out. The boy was five years old, weighed less than sixteen pounds, and was two feet tall. His parents agreed to allow Barnum to exhibit their son for a period of four weeks at three dollars a week. Barnum paid for their travel expenses to New York City. When they arrived on Thanksgiving Day, 1842, Barnum noted that "Mrs. Stratton was greatly astonished to find her son heralded in my Museum bills as General Tom Thumb, a dwarf of eleven years of age, just arrived from England!"

After the four weeks, Charles Stratton's parents signed another contract, this time for a year and much more money. Over the course of the year, Tom Thumb became quite famous. He and his parents toured America and Europe with Barnum. In 1863, Tom Thumb's marriage to Lavinia Warren, also a midget in Barnum's show, generated so much excitement that crowds thronged to Grace Episcopal Church on Broadway just to get a glimpse of the happy couple. Even today, Tom Thumb's boots and wedding jacket are displayed in museums.

Without question, Barnum exploited the public and his living curiosities, too. Yet, there is another side to the humbug scheme. The "curiosities" complied with Barnum's deceptions and they were paid well for exhibiting themselves. The "Wild Men of Borneo" (really Hiram and Barney Davis, both three and a half feet tall, born on a farm on Long Island, New York) earned $200,000 from exhibiting themselves with Barnum.

As for the public, they, too, played a role in the humbug.

"Illusion is a public need," Barnum once said. People want to be entertained and they don't care if the show is a hoax. As long as the public was willing to pay admission, *Barnum* would be the sucker for not giving them what they wanted.

MUTANT CHICKENS, CHOCOLATE CHIP COOKIES, AND SPAM

The Serious and Not-So-Serious Side of Media Hoaxes

The fast-food chain known until 1991 as Kentucky Fried Chicken was under investigation. Inspectors from the U. S. Food and Drug Administration had discovered that scientists working for Kentucky Fried Chicken on its poultry farms were genetically breeding birds with extra-large breasts and multiple legs—as many as eight! The government warned the company that these "mutant" birds could not be called chickens. To avoid heavy legal fines, Kentucky Fried Chicken changed its name to KFC.

At least, that's one version of the story that can be found on the Internet. The KFC Mutant Chicken is an urban legend, which means it isn't true…even if it is printed in more than one web site. Kentucky Fried Chicken did indeed change its name, but not because of a government threat. Here is the real reason: The state of Kentucky had recently trademarked its name. Now they were demanding royalties from all businesses that were using the name *Kentucky*. The "Colonel" refused. Instead of paying royalties, the company changed its name to

The Colonel could stay, said KFC's advertising bigwigs, but "Fried" had to go.

KFC. But even that explanation may not be true. According to a KFC spokesperson, the company wanted to take advantage of the public's growing concern with health and fitness. "The name 'Fried' is very limiting," said advertising vice president Peter Foulds in 1991. "What we want to do is take Kentucky Fried Chicken into the 90s and fit into consumers' lifestyles."

Hoaxes and urban legends are like echoes; they keep repeating. The person relaying the legend swears that it is true, having heard it from a "friend of a friend" who read it on the Internet or heard it on the radio. The story is passed on and on, either through word of mouth or through the media. Hundreds of hoaxes are zipping along the information superhighway, in particular. The "Neiman Marcus Cookie Caper" is one. Here is how it goes:

While shopping at a Neiman Marcus department store, a woman purchased a chocolate chip cookie. She thought it so delicious that she asked the clerk for the recipe. The clerk laughed and said it happened all the time and then handed the woman the cookie recipe on a preprinted sheet. The next month the shopper found that Neiman Marcus had

charged a $250 fee to her account for the recipe. Feeling
angry and betrayed, the woman is now sending the recipe
via the Internet to everyone she knows and asking them to
send it to everyone they know in order to prevent Neiman
Marcus from taking advantage of others as they had taken
advantage of her!

This sort of hoax is called spamming. That term refers specifically to the practice of sending as many junk E-mail messages and advertisements as possible over the Internet.

> To spam is to hoax fellow Internet
> users into repeating a bogus message. Spam
> also refers to any junk E-mail.

Neiman Marcus, however, calls the story "the cookie that will not crumble." The story just isn't true, says store representative Kellie Patrick. Here is why: Neiman Marcus doesn't bake cookies or sell them and so does not have a "unique" recipe. Besides, a charge cannot be made to a person's credit account without the person either signing a receipt or providing key information from the card, including account number and expiration date.

Often there is a history to these fictitious stories, and the resurfacing of a story is one hint that it may be a fake. Fifty years before Neiman Marcus was supposedly overcharging customers for a cookie recipe, the famous Waldorf-Astoria Hotel in New York City supposedly—according to the circulating legend at the time—was doing exactly the same thing with their red velvet cake recipe. Of course, there wasn't an Internet in the 1940s and 1950s, but there were chain letters (which work similarly to spamming) and that is how the red velvet recipe circled the globe.

Fabrications about mutant chickens, chocolate chip cookies, and red velvet cakes may seem harmless, but there is a serious side to these media-transmitted hoaxes. They often mirror the fears and obsessions that society harbors. The kernel of truth in the KFC hoax, for example, is that some scientists *really are* genetically altering foods, in some cases to create disease-resistant fruits and vegetables; in other instances, to develop new kinds of foods. The kernel of truth is what triggers the fear that gives rise to the legend.

Another serious side effect occurs when the news media becomes the unknowing target of a hoax. Each reported story that later proves to be false damages the media's credibility for reporting information accurately. The August 1998 shooting at the United States Capitol Building in Washington, D.C., and the hoax that followed afterward is an example.

On that summer day, Russell E. Weston, Jr., entered the Capitol Building and opened fire. He killed two capitol police officers and wounded a tourist before he himself fell in the exchange of gunfire. During CNN's live broadcast of the shooting, the station received what seemed like a very important telephone call. The caller claimed he represented the hospital where the injured assassin had been taken for emergency treatment. The show's producer plugged the call into the on-air commentator, Bernard Shaw.

Russell Weston had died, the hospital spokesman announced on the live broadcast. Clearly this was an opportune moment for Shaw and CNN—an exclusive report on the latest developments in the case. Shaw therefore engaged the caller in further conversation, asking him to speculate on the killer's motives. Weston was angry, the caller explained. "His radio was broken and he couldn't listen to Howard Stern."

Shaw immediately hung up. Howard Stern is an outspoken radio personality who has often shocked Americans with his publicity stunts.

Whoever had called CNN—it was not Howard Stern and it most definitely was not a hospital spokesman—the call was an embarrassment to the television network. The caller hoaxed CNN during a live broadcast about a tragic event. Russell Weston was not dead and his motive for the shooting had no relation to Howard Stern. The "joke" was in bad taste. More importantly, because the caller had somehow slipped through the otherwise tight net of people at CNN who screen crank calls, the incident damaged, if only a little, CNN's reputation as a trustworthy news source. Bernard Shaw apologized to his viewers. The broadcast continued.

Other recent stories reported by the media that have turned out to be hoaxes include these:

- *a 1990s* NBC Nightly News *brief in which the commentator said, "Scientists have discovered that some brands of kitty litter are radioactive." Not true. The story was a misread quote from another source about a single cat in Berkeley, California, that had somehow swallowed a dose of Iodine 131, a radioactive substance.*

- *a story in a Valdez, Alaska, newspaper that a bald eagle had swooped down into a gas station parking lot and "snatched" a "Chihuahua-like dog" that had been let out for some quick exercise by the owner of a motor home while he was refueling his vehicle. The wife was distraught. The husband silently cheered. Not true. The story has appeared many times elsewhere with different breeds of small dogs: poodles and Yorkshire terriers, for example.*

- *David Hartman, formerly of ABC's* Good Morning, America *interviewed on the television morning program a man named Joe Bones, founder of a business that helped people lose weight. When hired, his "fat squad" moved into the patron's house and forcibly prevented them from eating. Included on the program was a woman who "testified" that Joe Bones had helped her to lose a hundred pounds.* The Washington Post *and* The Philadelphia Inquirer *also covered the story, which was a hoax. The woman was a professional actress and Joe Bones was really Joey Scaggs, a man who hoaxes the media, he said, to prove that they are irresponsible in verifying their sources.*

■ ■ ■ ■   *a New Year's Day, 1998, story reported over Reuters, an organization that collects news stories and provides them to other news outlets. This one, "picked up" by CNN reported that the dog of a Pennsylvania woman had eaten a small cell phone that was a gift she had placed under her Christmas tree. The woman hadn't missed the phone until it started ringing—inside Charlie, her bloodhound. Not true.*

How this one started isn't known. Perhaps it was, after all, planted by some bored reporter who had to work on New Year's Eve.

BACK TO BARNUM: WHO ARE THE TASADY?

Why "Wish News" Gets Ink

Sometimes a story comes along that is so different or so exciting that a news editor wishes it were true. Harry Reichenbach, a press agent of the 1930s and 1940s, called such stories "wish news."

The editors of *National Geographic* were doing more than wishing, however, when they published a cover story in December 1971 on the mysterious Tasady people. According to the Philippine government, ruled then by dictator Ferdinand Marcos, the Tasady were a cave-dwelling tribe that lived in the highland rainforest on the Philippine island of Mindanao. Naked and using Stone Age tools made of bamboo, they lived peacefully quiet lives until a trapper from a neighboring tribe "stumbled" upon them. Isolated by mountains, the people knew nothing of the sea that surrounded their island or of the modern world beyond the sea. Nor did the modern world have any knowledge of them prior to 1971.

For more than a hundred years, The National Geographic Society has studied and written about world populations. The society has spon-

Tasady, or not Tasady? From left to right are Addg, Dul, Lolo, Gintoy, and Bilangen, members of a tribe of cave dwellers "discovered" in the Philippines in 1971, or so it was thought by the National Geographic Society.

sored expeditions to all corners of the globe in search of information to broaden knowledge of people's complex relationships. In the society's words, the Tasady provided a "rare opportunity of studying firsthand a people who…have lived in isolation for hundreds of years."

Scientists and writers from around the world, including a team from The National Geographic Society, traveled to Mindanao. They met with the Tasady. They could not speak their language, of course, but they could observe and photograph them and offer them token gifts never before seen by the Tasady—mirrors, metal knives. Fascinating details emerged. The Tasady had no word for "sea," having never seen the ocean. Nor had they ever seen the moon, because the tropical forest canopy on the island was so thick. Armed with field notes and photographs, the society published its cover story in December 1971.

After the first months of excitement over this amazing discovery, the Marcos government declared the Tasady's rich rainforest land "off limits to loggers, miners, and ranchers." It was a move that many scientists applauded. As the *National Geographic* article explained, "Without such help, the tribe—numbering perhaps a hundred in all—could disappear entirely."

In a way, they did disappear, for the Marcos government also banned all research and visits from foreigners. The Tasady were no longer in world newspaper headlines, though some journalists and researchers did not forget.

Years later in the mid-1980s, the story of the Tasady resurfaced after the death of Ferdinand Marcos. A Swiss journalist named Oswalk Iten returned to the caves of the Tasady and found them deserted. When Iten questioned the people of the neighboring tribe, they told him that the Tasady were really members of the Manubo-Blit tribe. Upon the urging of the Marcos government, they had posed as prehistoric people for the benefit of the researchers' cameras.

Reporters for a German magazine also returned to the island in the mid-1980s. They reported similar findings, but they left with something more: photographs of native people in modern dress—including a young man wearing a T-shirt with the American clothing label "Levi's" printed across the front. The man in the Levi's T-shirt had been photographed more than ten years earlier, naked and carrying a hammer of chipped stone tied with rattan to a wooden handle.

Were the Tasady truly a primitive people? Or were they a well-planned, well-rehearsed hoax? If it was a hoax, one so convincing that it fooled even the respected National Geographic Society, what was its purpose?

The answer may lie in the four books about the history of the Philippine culture written by Ferdinand Marcos at the time. Perhaps Marcos wished to instill pride in his people of their cultural heritage—even if he had to reinvent some of that heritage. Or perhaps he simply longed for the media spotlight to shine on him and his country. Perhaps the Tasady were, after all, his "wish news."

CHILDREN FROM HIS BRAIN

L. Frank Baum was a media wizard, too, even before he wrote *The Wonderful Wizard of Oz.* He created shop window displays for large department stores. Window shopping wasn't an American pastime in the 1890s, but the invention of plate glass— and L. Frank Baum's imagination—changed all that. To arouse interest in passers-by in the street, Baum created fantastic scenes behind the glass. Electric lights, gadgets that twisted and twirled, mechanical birds and butterflies, and Ferris wheels…Baum's window display was like a miniature Oz. But could he get people to actually stop and notice the wonderful world in the window? He hired people to walk by and stop and stare and "Ooooh" and "Aaaahhh!" Naturally, others who passed by were intrigued—what was all the fuss about? They stopped, too. "It is said that people are not readily deceived by window displays," Baum later wrote, "but we all know better than that." [12]

But it was Baum's Oz characters—the Scarecrow, the Tin Man, Dorothy, and the Wizard—that he loved best. He called them the "children from his brain." Published in 1900, *The Wonderful Wizard of Oz* was an immediate hit, a best-selling book that earned Baum some much-needed money and a reputation as a children's author. He gave up window dressing but not media wizardry. Two years later Baum rewrote Oz as a musical for the stage. Like Oz the Great and Terrible, Baum thought up illusions to fascinate his audience—twirling lights and storm clouds projected on a green curtain gave the audience the thrilling impression of a cyclone on stage. When the play opened, Baum sat in the theater and watched the stuff of his imagination come to life. Afterward in an interview, he described how he felt:

"The appearance of the Tin Woodman made me catch my breath spasmodically and when the gorgeous poppy field, with its human flowers, burst on my view—more real than my fondest dreams had ever conceived—a big lump came into my throat and a wave of gratitude swept over me that I had lived to see the sight. I cannot be ashamed of these emotions."[13]

L. Frank Baum died before he saw his story and the children from his brain projected through still another medium: motion pictures. The 1939 release of *The Wizard of Oz* is considered today a media classic.

Are media manipulations a bad thing? Baum didn't think so. He truly believed that the children from his brain brought happiness to millions of people. Like Oz, media wizards when they are making believe can be terrible. But they can also, at times, be

great.

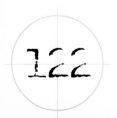

Revealing the Wizard

CHAPTER NOTES

INTRODUCTION
1. L. Frank Baum, *The Annotated Wizard of Oz* (New York: Clarkson N. Potter, 1973), 134.

PART ONE
2. Ben Bradlee, *A Good Life: Newspapering and Other Adventures* (New York: Simon & Schuster, 1995), 456.
3. Reed Irvine and Cliff Kincaid, "How Lies Get Into the Media," *Media Monitor*, August 11, 1998.
4. Mike Sager, "Janet's World," *Gentleman's Quarterly*, September 1996, 208.
5. Parsons Weems, *A History of the Life and Death, Virtues and Exploits of General George Washington* (Philadelphia: Lippincott, 1918), 23.
6. "An Anchor's Perspective on Critical TV Viewing," *ABC Classroom Connection* (Newtown, PA: ABC Television, 1993), 3.
7. All quotes attributed to Gardner come from the Library of Congress American Memory files.

PART THREE
8. Howard Kurtz, *Hot Air: All Talk All the Time* (New York: Times Books, Random House, 1996), 66.
9. National Public Radio, "Talk of the Nation" August 12, 1998.
10. Michael Crichton, interview posted on Ultimate TV website, October 1998.

PART FOUR
11. *USA Today*, March 27, 1991, 4B.

EPILOGUE
12. David Traxel, *1898: The Birth of the American Century* (New York: Alfred A. Knopf, 1998), 302.
13. Baum, 49, quoting a 1903 New York newspaper interview.

SELECTED SOURCES

ABC Classroom Connection. Newtown, PA: ABC Television, 1993.

Baum, L. Frank. *The Annotated Wizard of Oz*. New York: Clarkson N. Potter, 1973.

Begley, Sharon and Debbie Seward. "Back From the Stone Age?" *Newsweek* 107:69, May 5, 1986.

Berneys, Edward L. *Crystallizing Public Opinion*. New York: Liveright Publishing, 1923.

Bradlee, Ben. *A Good Life: Newspapering and Other Adventures*. New York: Simon & Schuster, 1995.

Bradley, William. "Perspectives on the Election" *Los Angeles Times*, November 6, 1996.

Browne, Waldo R. *Barnum's Own Story: The Autobiography of P. T. Barnum*. Gloucester, MA: Peter Smith Publishing, 1972. Reprint of the Viking Press edition, 1927.

Carnes, Mark C., ed. *Past Imperfect: History According to the Movies*. New York: Henry Holt, 1995.

Clark, Eric. *The Want Makers: The World of Advertising; How They Make You Buy*. New York: Viking, 1988.

Collins, James. "Talking Trash." *Time*, March 30, 1998.

Enrico, Dottie. "Mountain Dew's Hip Ads Refresh Viewers," *USA Today*, May 18, 1998.

Enrico, Dottie. "Pepsi Hits the Spot with Super Bowl Ads," *USA Today*, January 29, 1996.

Farquhar, Michael. "And the Hoaxes Just Keep Coming." *The Los Angeles Times*, December 13, 1996.

"First Glimpse of a Stone Age Tribe." *National Geographic*, Vol. 140, December 1971.

Forman, Ross. "The Ross Report." World Champion Wrestling website, December 19, 1997 posting.

Fuhrman, Cadic Jacobson. *Publicity Stunt: Great Staged Events That Made the News*. San Francisco: Chronicle Books, 1989.

Garner, Dwight. "Beg, Borrow, or . . ." *Salon Magazine* (online), September 2, 1998 posting.

Garner, Dwight. "Violence or Entertainment?" *Salon Magazine* (online), August 17, 1998 posting.

Gartner, Michael. "Why Risk 'Enhancing' News?" *USA Today*, June 28, 1994.

Gross, Linden. " 'ER' Behind the Scenes." *Reader's Digest*, April, 1998.

Hallin, Danile C. "Sound Bite News: Television Coverage of Elections, 1968-1988." *Journal of Communication,* Spring 1992.

"Harassed to Death?" *20/20,* ABC News website, September 16, 1998 posting.

Hine, Thomas. *The Total Package: The Evolution and Secret Meaning of Boxes, Bottles, Cans & Tubes.* New York: Little, Brown, 1995.

Igengar, Shanto. *Is Anyone Responsible? How TV Frames Political Issues.* Chicago: University of Chicago Press, 1991.

Jackson, Janine and Jim Naureckas. "Crime Contradictions." *EXTRA!* From FAIR website, May/June 1994 posting.

Jacobson, Michael F. and Laurie Ann Mazur. *Marketing Madness: A Survival Guide for a Consumer Society.* San Francisco: Westview Press, 1995.

Jensen, Elizabeth, D.M., et. al. "Consumer Alert." *Brill's Content*, October 1998.

"The Jordan Phenomenon." *The News Hour with Jim Lehrer*, June 15, 1998.

Kelly, Kevin. "Beneath the Skin with Chyna." *World Wrestling Federation Magazine*, October 1998.

Kelly, Kevin. "Champion of the Disabled . . . Or the Deceitful?" *World Wrestling Federation Magazine,* October 1998.

Kurtz, Howard. *Hot Air: All Talk All the Time.* NY: Times Books, Random House, 1996.

Lacayo, Richard. "Toward the Root of the Evil." *Time*, April 6, 1998.

Lacayo, Richard and George Russell. *Eyewitness: 15 Years of Photojournalism.* New York: The Time Inc. Magazine Co., 1995.

Library of Congress's American Memory (online). "Does the Camera Ever Lie?;" "The Case of the Confused Identity;" "The Case of the Moved Body."

Lichter, S. Robert et. al. *The Media Elite.* Bethesda, MD: Adler and Adler, 1986.

Martin, Chuck. "Boo! Which Scary Food or Drink is the Latest Nutritional Goblin?" *The Cincinnati Enquirer*, October 19, 1996.

National Public Radio interview with Larry Tye, author of *Father of Spin.* August 25, 1998. Host: Renee Montagne.

Negroni, Christine. "Media Are Victims of Hoax." CNN website, January 30, 1996 posting.

Peterson, Tricia. "Gartner Recaps Career in Newspapers, TV News." *Newseum* Online, September 24, 1997.

Picard, Robert G. *Media Portrayals of Terrorism Function and Meaning of News Coverage.* Ames: Iowa University Press, 1993.

"Popcorn Tins, Aprons, Valentines and Bandages All Look Like Mike." *Wall Street Journal*, November 15, 1996.

Preston, Ivan L. *The Great American Blowup: Puffery in Advertising and Selling.* Madison: University of Wisconsin Press, 1996.

Pungente, John J., SJ, director. *Scanning Television: Videos for Media Literacy in Class.* Face to Face Media and the Jesuit Communication Project, 1997. Teacher's Guide by Neil Andersen and John J. Pungente, SJ. Toronto: Harcourt, Brace Canada, 1997. From video 2: "Public Service Announcements," "No Smoking!" From Video 3: "Niketown," "Wrestling for Dollars."

"Report: Philip Morris Polled Teens on Smoking." CNN Interactive website, December 15, 1996 posting.

Rose, Ted. "The Hunters: How Television Bookers Get their Men (and Women and Children)." *Brill's Content*, August 1998.

Sager, Mike. "Janet's World." *Gentleman's Quarterly*, September 1996.

Sawyer, Diane, moderater. "3,000 Minutes." *The New York Times Magazine*, September 20, 1998.

"Shaping and Reshaping the Tasady: A Question of Cultural Identity." *Journal of Asian Studies*, August 1991.

"Shaq Returns to the School Playground to Star in Pepsi's 'Bench.'" PepsiCo Press Release, April 2, 1998.

Smith, Jane Webb. *Smoke Signals: Cigarette Advertising and the American Way of Life.* Chapel Hill: University of North Carolina Press, 1990.

Stein, Joel. "The One and Only." *Time*, June 22, 1998.

Stossel, Scott. "The Man Who Counts the Killings." *Atlantic Monthly*, May 1997.

Traxel, David. *1898: The Birth of the American Century*. New York: Alfred A. Knopf, 1998.

"Tumulty Letter in Press Agent Inquiry." *New York Times*, July 30, 1920.

Ultimate TV website: Real Player interviews with Michael Crichton, Anthony Edwards, and Noah Wiley, September 1998 posting.

"Violent Schools: Perception or Reality?" CNN website, August 24, 1998 posting.

Weems, Parsons. *A History of the Life and Death, Virtues and Exploits of General George Washington.* Philadelphia: Lippincott, 1918.

Index

Page numbers in *italics*
refer to illustrations.

Aaron, Charles, 80, 81
Abdul, Paula, 62
advertising, 9, 43–52
    holidays and, 53–58
    law and, 65–69
    subtexts, 59–64
ambushing, 17
American Airlines, 66
American Civil War, 12, *28*, 29–32,
    33, 34
American Museum, 104–106, *107*
American Tobacco Company, 47
Associated Press (AP), 76

Barnum, P.T., 101, 103–106, 109–
    110
Barrett, Stephen, 83
Baum, Harry, 7–8
Baum, L. Frank, 7–9, 101, 121–122
Bergen, Candice, 62
Bernays, Edward L., 44–45, 47, 48,
    51, 52
bias, 21–25, 27
bookers, 76
Bounty paper towel, 62
Bradlee, Ben, 16
Brady, Matthew, 29
breaking news, 76, 80, 85

Center for Media and Public
    Affairs, 73
chain letters, 113
Chandler, Asa, 63
Chang and Eng, 106

Cheskin, Louis, 42–43
Chesterfield cigarettes, 47–49
Christian Century, The, 49
Christmas, 53, 55
Chyna, 93–94, 97
cigarette smoking, 47–49, *50*, 51–52
Clinton, Bill, 24, 25
Clinton, Hillary Rodham, 25, *26*
Cloffulia, Madame Josephine, 106
CNN, 76, 77, *79*, 81, 114–115
Coca-Cola, 63–64, *65*
code words, 12–13, 17, 48
Committee on Public Information
    (CPI), 44
composites, 12–13
composition of photograph, 31, 34
Cooke, Janet, *14*, 15–16, 20
copywriters, 55–58
Crichton, Michael, 91, 92

Dateline (television show), 19
deceptive advertising, 65–69
demonstration ads, 60, 62, 63
Dole, Bob, 25, 27

Edwards, Anthony, *88*, 89, 92
episodic reporting, 77, 78, 80, 81
ER (television show), *88*, 89–92

Federal Trade Commission (FTC),
    65–66, 68–69
FeeJee Maiden, 105–106
feeling ads, 56
54th Massachusetts Volunteer
    Regiment, 12
Foulds, Peter, 112
frame, 17–18, 77–78, 81

Frassanito, William, 31, 32
Frosted Mini Wheats, 67

Garbarino, James, 80–81
Gardner, Alexander, 29–32, 34
Gartner, Michael, 13, 18–20
General Motors (GM), 19–20
Gettysburg, Battle of, *28*, 29–32,
    33, 34
Glory (film), 12–13
Golden, Andrew, 75, 76, 80, 81
Goldman, Ronald, 16

Halloween, 55
Hanes underwear, 62
Hanukkah, 55
Hart, Mike "The Hitman," 94, 96
Hartman, David, 115
headlines, 25
Heth, Joice, 103–104
Hewitt, Don, 83, 86
hoaxes (urban legends), 100–101,
    103–106, 109–116
Hogan, Hulk, *95*
holidays, 53–58
humbugs, 104, 109, 110

infotainment, 84, 87
interactive experience, 63–64
Irving, Washington, 53
Iten, Oswalk, 119
It Takes a Village (H. Clinton), 25,
    26
Ivory Soap, *46*, 47

Jarre, Kevin, 12
Jennings, Peter, 27

Jenny (television talk show), 17
JFK (film), 17–18
"Jimmy's World" (Cooke), *14*, 15–16, 20
Johnson, Mitchell, 75, 77, 80, 81
JoJo the Dog-Faced Boy, 106
jolts per minute (JPMs), 73, 90
Jonesboro shooting, *74*, 75–78, 80–81
Jordan, Michael, 62

Kelly, Kevin, 96
Kennedy, John F., 17
Kentucky Fried Chicken, 111–112, *112*, 114
Kwanzaa, 55

Lake, Ricki, 72, 73
Lazarus, Fred, Jr., 55
Lee, Ivy, 45, 52
lifestyle ads, 59–60, *61*, 63
Lucky Strike cigarettes, *50*

Marcos, Ferdinand, 117, 119, 120
marketers, 55–58
market share, 91
Marlboro cigarettes, 47, 49
McDonald's, 69
McDonald's Quarter Pounder, 66–67
MCI, 62
McPherson, James, 13
media metaphors, 35–39
mock-ups, 67–68
montage, 18, 91
Moore, Clement Clarke, 53
Moore, Martha T., 69
Mountain Dew, 59–60, *61*

Nast, Thomas, 53, *54*
National Geographic Society, 117, 119, 120
Neiman Marcus, 112–113
newsmagazines, 82–86
Niketown, 63

O'Donnell, Rosie, 57
O'Sullivan, Timothy, 32, 34

out of context, 25, 27
over acts, 47

Patrick, Kellie, 113
Pepsico Inc., 59
photo-illustration, 17
piping, 16
presidential elections, 24, 25
press agents, 45, 51, 52
Preston, Ivan, 66
product packaging, 42–43
propaganda, 44, 45
public relations, 47
public service announcement (PSA), 35–39, *38*
puffery, 66, 69

Quinones, John, 85

radio, 24
Reader's Digest, 51
Reebok sneakers, 62
Reichenbach, Harry, 45, 51, 52, 117
Rockefeller, John D., 45, *46*, 52
Roosevelt, Franklin D., 55

Safer, Morley, 82, 83, 85
Sager, Mike, 20
Sandburg, Carl, 36
Santa Claus, 53, *54*, 55
Scaggs, Joey, 116
scare tactics, 82–87
segment producers, 76
sensation transference, 42–43
Shaw, Bernard, 114, 115
Shaw, Robert Gould, 12, 13
Simpson, Nicole Brown, 16
Simpson, O.J., 16, *17*
60 Minutes (newsmagazine), 82–83, 86
slice-of-life ads, 60, 63
sound bites, 9, 24–25
spamming, 113
Springer, Jerry, 72, *73*
Stern, Howard, 114–115
Stone, Oliver, 17–18

Suarez, Ray, 80
subtexts, 59–64
Super Bowl Sunday, 68–69
super weasels, 68–69
"Swimmers" (public service announcement), 35–39, *38*

talking heads, 77
Tasady people, 117, *118*, 119–120
teasers, 25
testimonials, 62, 63
Thanksgiving, 55
thematic reporting, 77, 78, 80, 81
thinking ads, 56
Thumb, General Tom, *108*, 109
Tickle Me Elmo, 57–58
Tide laundry detergent, 43
tight shot, 19
Time magazine, 16–17
20/20 (newsmagazine), 83
Tyco toy company, 57

Ventura, Jesse "The Body," *95*
Viceroy cigarettes, 51–52
Vickers & Benson, 35–37, 39
Volvo, 65, 68–69

Waldorf-Astoria Hotel, New York, 113
Warren, Lavinia, *108*, 109
Washington, George, 21–25, 103, 104
Washington Post, 15, 16, 20
Waters, Lou, 76
weasels, 66–68
Weems, Parsons, 21–25, 27
Weston, Russell E., Jr., 114–115
Wild Men of Borneo, 110
wish news, 117, 120
Wizard of Oz, The (film), *9*, 122
Wonderful Wizard of Oz, The (Baum), *6*, 7–9, 121–122
World War I, 44, 47
wrestling, 93–94, *95*, 96–97
Wyle, Noah, 92